THE PRESIDENCY

OF

GEORGE WASHINGTON

JACK D. WARREN, JR.

FOREWORD BY GEORGE H. W. BUSH

THIS PUBLICATION WAS MADE POSSIBLE BY

ANN L. BROWNSON

Mount Vernon Ladies' Association
Mount Vernon, Virginia 22121

The Mount Vernon Ladies' Association
P.O. Box 110
Mount Vernon, Virginia 22121

Cover illustration:
portrait by Gilbert Stuart,

Library of Congress Cataloging-in-Publication Data

Warren, Jack D.
The Presidency of George Washington / Jack D. Warren, Jr., written especially
for the Mount Vernon Ladies' Association of the Union.
p. cm.
"This book is a much-expanded version of a paper presented in
November 1996 to the first annual Mount Vernon Symposium on
George Washington." Includes bibliographical references and index.
ISBN 0-931917-34-4

1. Washington, George, 1732-1799. 2. United States–Politics and
Government, 1789-1797. I. Mount Vernon Ladies' Association of the
Union. II. Title.
E311. W37 2000
973.4'1'092–dc21   00-011662

For Emily,
Audrey, and Jack

Heirs to
Washington's Republic

TABLE OF CONTENTS

FOREWORD

EACH OF OUR PAST PRESIDENTS HAS started his term of office with a wide range of challenging issues already on the table, and you can rest assured that unexpected problems always arise at a moment's notice. But only one man has been forced to face these problems without the benefit of past examples, both good and bad. George Washington was first, and how fortunate we are that an individual of such remarkable character and leadership was thrust into this role.

Interestingly, Washington was so uniquely qualified to serve as first president in large part because the office itself was structured with him in mind. Only Washington had the support of both southerners and northerners, both merchants and farmers, both soldiers and civilians. He was the one person who could be trusted in this new position of chief executive, and over a span of two terms, he seldom fell short of the people's very high expectations.

Washington had many traits that made him an ideal first president. His integrity was totally inflexible, his judgment was solid, his sense of fairness was legendary, and he followed one simple rule—in every decision, he tried to do what was best for his country.

Washington set a number of important precedents which continue to stand today, and modern leaders still admire his skills as a negotiator, an administrator and an inspirational leader of the entire nation. But most of all, we can look up to George Washington, the man. The presidency did not shape George Washington—his character was so established and so strong that he knew instinctively where to set the appropriate boundaries, and how to be a strong and effective leader. He shaped the presidency into one of the most powerful positions in the world, yet never wavered from his promise to remain a servant of the people.

Although praise poured down on Washington from all corners of the nation, he somehow maintained a genuine sense of modesty. The poet Robert Frost was exactly right when he said, "George Washington was one of the few in the whole history of the world who was not carried away by power."

As Washington realized more than 200 years ago, serving as President of the United States is a privilege like none other. And for the men and women who have followed and will attempt to follow in President Washington's impressive footsteps, one of the greatest honors of all is trying to live up to the standards established by our first president. Although few may ultimately achieve this lofty goal, there is something to be said for setting the bar so high. The life and legacies of Washington should inspire all presidents, and in fact all Americans, for many generations still to come.

George Bush

ACKNOWLEDGMENTS

THIS BOOK IS A MUCH-EXPANDED version of a paper presented in November 1996 to the first annual Mount Vernon Symposium on George Washington, an event made possible through the generous support of the Barra Foundation. Special thanks are due Richard Norton Smith, the moderator on that occasion, and the other participants especially Kenneth Bowling, Peter Henriques, Richard Brookhiser, and Roger Brown, who offered useful challenges and cautionary advice, as well as to James Rees, Executive Director of Mount Vernon, and his staff for mounting the event and bringing together such an engaging group of historians. John Riley, former Historian of Mount Vernon, challenged me to attempt this broader reinterpretation of the Washington presidency. A portion of the manuscript was presented in the Liberty Lecture Series at Gunston Hall, where Thomas Lainhoff and Linda Hartman were gracious hosts. Bill Beck and Lynne Warren offered important assistance in developing the manuscript. Peter Henriques, Kenneth Bowling, and Frank Grizzard read the entire manuscript and offered useful advice. My appreciation is due most of all to my friends Dorothy Twohig and Mark Mastromarino formerly of The Papers of George Washington Project at the University of Virginia, in whose company I was privileged to spend five years editing Washington's presidential papers for publication.

JDW

PROLOGUE
A RELUCTANT DEPARTURE

GEORGE WASHINGTON RECORDED IN HIS DIARY for April 16, 1789, that "About ten o'clock I bade adieu to Mount Vernon, to private life, and to domestic felicity; and with a mind oppressed with more anxious and painful sensations than I have words to express, set out for New York ... with the best dispositions to render service to my country in obedience to its call, but with less hope of answering its expectations."[1]

Washington had been informed of his election as first President under the new Federal Constitution two days earlier by Charles Thomson, the secretary of Congress, who arrived at Mount Vernon bearing a letter from John Langdon, President *pro tem* of the new Senate. Langdon had opened the ballots on April 6 and found that every elector had cast a vote for Washington. He remains the only President in American history to be elected by the unanimous voice of the people.

The news came to Mount Vernon as no surprise. Washington had known his election was certain for months, and was already completing preparations to leave Mount Vernon for New York City, where the new Congress had convened. Yet he did so, he explained in a letter to his old friend Henry Knox, like "a culprit who is going to the place of his execution, so unwilling am I, in the evening of a life nearly consumed in public cares, to quit a peaceful abode for an Ocean of difficulties."[2]

Why then, did he do it? Why did he come out of retirement to accept an office that he knew would present difficulties and challenges as great as any he had faced in the Revolutionary War?

He unquestionably had personal motives, but the obvious ones— hunger for fame, power, or financial reward—were not among them. In 1789 Washington was already one of the most famous men in the world—celebrated in Europe and America as the living embodiment of

West façade of Mount Vernon. Called from retirement at his beloved Mount Vernon, Washington departed for New York City to assume the presidency in April 1789.

a classical hero. He had led the American army to a victory that was widely regarded as miraculous. At the close of the Revolutionary War sweeping powers had been within his reach, but he had spurned them, resigning his commission and returning to Mount Vernon without claiming any reward for his services. At a time when other men were willing to convulse whole continents to gain power, Washington's conduct astonished the world. His reputation, as he understood better than anyone, rested on his refusal to grasp at power. Accepting the presidency could not add luster to this reputation, and was almost certain to tarnish it.

The presidency held out utterly no prospect of financial gain. Years of public service had already left Washington's personal finances in disarray. On the eve of the Revolution, Washington had been well on his way to making Mount Vernon one of the most productive plantations in Virginia, and himself one of the wealthiest planters in the colony. Eight years of neglect while he served at the head of the Continental Army had left the estate in shambles. In 1789 Washington was still working to recover his shattered fortunes and rebuild his plantation. He had to borrow £500 from an Alexandria merchant to pay his debts and make the trip to New York for his inauguration. The presidency required long absences from Mount Vernon and foreclosed any possibility that Washington would realize his ambition to make the estate a model of agricultural productivity. Worse, Washington's presidential salary never paid the costs of maintaining the presidential household and entertaining the constant stream of congressmen, foreign dignitaries, and other worthies who crowded his table. Although his salary—$25,000 a year—was several times more than that of other federal officials, the presidency involved a considerable financial sacrifice for Washington.[3]

Washington accepted the presidency because he believed that the nation was passing through a critical period that would decide whether it would "survive as an independent Republic, or decline . . . into insignificant & wretched fragments of Empire." The new Federal Constitution offered a chance—Washington believed it was a final chance—to preserve the Union and vindicate the republican form of government. At such a critical moment, Washington wrote, neither "the hazard to which my former reputation might be exposed, or the terror of encountering new fatigues & troubles" could deter him from answering the call of his country. "I would not seek or retain popularity," he told Henry Lee, "at the expence of one social duty or moral obligation."[4]

Washington had watched through the post-war years with mounting dismay as the weak Union created by the Articles of Confederation gradually disintegrated, becoming "a shadow without the substance." He was appalled by the excesses of the state legislatures—particularly the stay laws and paper money acts that defrauded creditors—angered by the popular licentiousness reflected most dramatically in Shays' Rebellion in Massachusetts, and frustrated by the diplomatic, financial, and military impotence of the Confederation Congress. "Illiberality, jealousy, and local policy mix too much in all our public councils for the good government of the Union" he complained. By 1786 Washington had concluded that reform was essential. "Thirteen Sovereignties pulling against each other," he wrote to James Madison, "and all tugging at the federal head, will soon bring ruin on the whole." What was needed, he argued, was an "energetic Constitution, well guarded & closely watched, to prevent incroachments" that would "restore us to that degree of respectability & consequence, to which we had a fair claim, & the brightest prospect of attaining."[5]

Under the new Federal Constitution Washington envisioned a great republic that would serve the interests of the American people and bind them together in an indissoluble Union, taking advantage of the natural and political circumstances of the United States to make its people free, powerful and prosperous. To achieve this aim, Washington was convinced that the United States must become an expansive, continental republic, an "empire of liberty," bound together by a government responsive to the popular will. This was a bold, even radical idea. Contemporary political thought held that popular governments were inherently weak. Washington was not a deep student of political history, but it did not take wide reading or long study to understand that republics had always been among the most fragile and ephemeral governments in the world. Nor did it require a profound scholar to know that European political theorists were almost all agreed that republican government could only survive in a small, socially homogeneous nation, where representatives were in close contact with their constituents and responsive to their will.

Washington denied that this reasoning applied to the United States. He was certain that an effective continental Union was the only realistic source of American strength and respectability. As the most experienced military man on the continent, Washington never lost sight of the fact that the individual states were powerless in a world of predatory powers.

The Union established by the Articles of Confederation was not strong enough to command the respect of European nations or even to provide the new nation with an adequate defense. Washington realized that nothing but a strengthened Union could prevent the states from engaging in suicidal commercial warfare or from adopting disastrous fiscal policies to escape the burden of debts remaining from the Revolutionary War. An energetic Union was the only hope for establishing the new nation's finances on a sound footing, and the only thing that could prevent the country from breaking apart into rival confederacies.

Washington's determination to secure the Union defined his presidency. While Washington did not assume the presidency with a legislative agenda, like a modern president, he did have a series of goals for the new government—all of which he believed were essential to his broader purpose of securing the Union—and all of which assumed a prominent place in his correspondence during the last years of the Confederation. "If I can form a plan for my own conduct," Washington wrote to Lafayette in January 1789, "my endeavours shall be unremittingly exerted (even at the hazard of former fame or present popularity) to extricate my country from the embarassments in which it is entangled, through want of credit; and to establish, a general system of policy, which, if pursued, will insure permanent felicity to the Commonwealth. I think, I see a path, as clear and as direct as a ray of light, which leads to the attainment of that object."[6]

Washington's first goal, upon which all the others depended, was the establishment of a government endowed with energy, capable of responding effectively to the domestic problems and foreign crises that threatened the new nation—a government led by men of unimpeachable character, whose honesty, integrity, and devotion to the republic would command the respect of the American people. The great challenge to this government was settling the outstanding Revolutionary debts of the Confederation government equitably, and establishing of the credit of the new federal government on a sound basis. Washington knew little about the principles of large-scale debt finance, but he understood that unless the outstanding debts of the Confederation were resolved, the nation's credit would be ruined.

His second goal was the final settlement of the treaty of peace with Britain, which meant most importantly securing control of the posts in the Northwest Territory still held by the British Army. Intertwined with this was the goal of pacifying the western frontier of the new nation and opening it up to American settlement. Connected with this was the opening of the Mississippi River, controlled by Spain, to American commerce. Finally, and perhaps most important for Washington, was the maintenance of peace. Washington, as Edmund Morgan has pointed out, "had ample experience that war was the way to poverty, and poverty meant impotence." Peace would give the new nation time to grow in population, economic power, and geographic extent—all of which would ultimately secure the strength and respectability of the United States and establish its place among nations.[7]

The obstacles Washington faced as he left Mount Vernon must have seemed almost insurmountable. "I anticipated," he wrote to an English friend, "in a heart filled with distress, the ten thousand embarrassments, perplexities and troubles to which I must again be exposed in the evening of a life, already nearly consumed in public cares." But Washington possessed the advantage of having the universal support of his countrymen. If he had any doubt of this fact, his eight-day trip to New York City must have reassured him. Signal cannons boomed and church bells rang as he rode northward, and at every stop he was met by official delegations, cavalry escorts, pageants, and great civic feasts. The popular outpouring of affection and support reached a climax when Washington reached New York. On April 23 a special barge ferried him across New York Harbor, followed by a procession of sailing ships. Salutes were fired, flags unfurled, and thousands of citizens packed the waterfront to get a glimpse of the arriving hero. The applause was gratifying, but Washington worried privately that "my countrymen will expect too much from me" and that the "extravagant (and I may say undue) praises which they are heaping upon me at this moment" would eventually turn into "equally extravagant (though I will fondly hope, unmerited) censures."[8]

A week later, on April 30, 1789, Washington appeared on the open portico of Federal Hall to the roar of applause and cheers from the crowd in the streets below, and took the oath of office. He then retired inside, and in a quiet voice, read his brief Inaugural Address to the members of Congress and other public officials. "It was a very touching scene," recorded Congressman Fisher Ames, "and quite of the solemn kind. His aspect grave, almost to sadness; his modesty, actually shaking; his voice deep, a little tremulous, and so low as to call for close attention." Washington explained his reluctance to accept the office and begged the indulgence of the American people if his "inferior endowments" and lack of experience in public administration led him

Washington took the oath of office on the open portico of New York's Federal Hall, overlooking Wall Street. After administering the oath, New York Chancellor Robert R. Livingston turned to the crowd and shouted "Long live George Washington, President of the United States!"

into error. He expressed his hope that no local attachments or partisan animosities would distract the government from serving the interests of the Union. "The preservation of the sacred fire of liberty and the destiny of the Republican model of Government," he said, "are justly considered as *deeply*, perhaps as *finally* staked on the experiment entrusted to the hands of the American people." For the following eight years, Washington dedicated himself completely to securing the Union. Others would hesitate, lose faith, or change course. Washington never wavered.[9]

CHAPTER ONE
THE EYES OF ARGUS

GEORGE WASHINGTON'S STATUS AS THE TRANSCENDENT hero of the American Revolution was not secured on the battlefield. It was secured at the conclusion of the war, when he appeared before Congress and returned his commission as commander of the victorious Continental Army. Washington's reputation was achieved by surrendering power. His willingness to do so inspired confidence, and led to his being entrusted with the most powerful executive office under the Federal Constitution. But in order to provide the new nation with effective executive leadership, Washington had to define the powers of the presidency, which were barely outlined in the Federal Constitution, and wield them with energy. Establishing the authority of the president without losing the confidence of Americans presented Washington with one of the greatest challenges of his presidency.

Americans of the Revolutionary generation were especially suspicious of executive power. The Revolutionary movement had been fueled by real and perceived abuses of executive authority—by customs officials, tax collectors, colonial governors, the distant colonial bureaucracy in London, the King's ministers, and ultimately, the King himself. In creating their own governments the revolutionaries had gone to great lengths to prevent the abuse of executive power—vesting executive authority in committees rather than individuals, weakening the power of governors, limiting the time individuals could hold executive offices, banning individuals from holding more than one office at a time, and by shifting executive authority to state and local governments, where alert citizens could keep watch over officials for signs of corruption. The government established by the Articles of Confederation had no independent executive branch at all.

Powel coach. *Elegant but not ostentatious, the Powel coach now at Mount Vernon is substantially the same as the one Washington used on his 1791 tour of the South.*

The convention that framed the Federal Constitution agreed that the establishment of a more effective executive branch was essential for the preservation of the Union, but its members were not immune to ideological anxiety about the abuse of executive power. They initially considered vesting executive authority in a committee. Once the decision was made to have a single executive, they debated the powers of the office at length before agreeing to invest a single president with the entire executive authority of the federal government. The convention only took this step because, as one of the delegates wrote, "many of the members cast their eyes towards General Washington as President; and shaped their Ideas of the Powers to be given to a President, by their opinions of his Virtue." Despite the faith that Americans had in Washington, suspicion of the energetic use of executive authority persisted under the Federal Constitution. "The doctrine of energy in Government," John Page declared on the floor of First Congress, "is the true doctrine of tyrants."[10]

Washington did not share this ideological preoccupation about the corrupting influence of executive power. He believed that executive authority, properly checked but concentrated in the hands of relatively few, was essential to effective government. But he understood that the presidency was on trial, and that every measure of his administration would be scrutinized closely. "My political conduct," Washington explained to his nephew Bushrod, "must be exceedingly circumspect and proof against just criticism, for the eyes of Argus are upon me, and no slip will pass unnoticed."[11]

Among Washington's most important accomplishments as president was establishing American confidence in strong executive leadership. Washington endowed the presidency with the dignity requisite for a head of state, while avoiding the ostentatiousness associated with monarchy. He administered the government with fairness, efficiency, and integrity, assuring Americans that the president could exercise broad executive authority without partiality, caprice, or corruption, and he executed the laws with justice and restraint, while convincing his countrymen that the energetic government need not become tyrannical. Within the first eighteen months of his presidency, Washington defined a standard of fitness for presidential appointments that marked a departure from the corrupt patronage employed by European governments, established the responsibility of the department heads to the president through a well-articulated administrative system, and demonstrated that an energetic executive did not have to encroach on the prerogatives of the legislature to provide effective leadership.

In the days after his inauguration, the press of invitations and the crowds of visitors seeking Washington's attention threatened to make it impossible for him to administer the government at all. He quickly concluded that he would have to establish formal procedures regulating his social life in order to have any time left to carry out his duties. After consulting with John Adams, John Jay, James Madison, and Alexander Hamilton, Washington decided to hold weekly levees at which to receive casual visitors. He also decided not to return visits or accept private dinner invitations

Washington's presidential travels helped secure popular attachment to the new nation.

and to limit his own entertaining to small groups. His purpose was not to glorify himself but to establish the dignity of his office and make it possible for him to accomplish the work he had been elected to perform.

A few critics—more as the administration progressed—charged that these policies imitated the forms of monarchy. The levees came in for much of the criticism. They were stiff, ceremonial affairs, at which callers were presented to the President and formed a circle around the room, after which Washington made his way around the circle and spoke briefly to as many of his visitors as he could. Any respectably dressed gentleman could attend one of these events; neither invitations nor letters of introduction were required. When he learned that prominent Virginians, including his neighbor George Mason, were saying that the levees were part of a conspiracy to surround the President with the pomp of royalty, Washington privately complained that he could not see "what pomp there is in all this." Perhaps, he mused sarcastically, "it consists in not sitting."

Such criticism frustrated Washington. He generally disliked being the object of public rituals and avoided them whenever possible. He privately insisted that he would rather "be at Mount Vernon with a friend or two about me than to be attended at the seat of government by the officers of state and the representatives of every power in Europe." He disapproved of proposals to invest the president with

11

aristocratic-sounding titles such as "His Elective Highness." He discouraged public festivities on his birthday, partly because such celebrations interfered with the public business, and partly because they were an imitation of the British custom of celebrating royal birthdays. His wishes, in this last respect, were invariably ignored.[12]

Although Washington had little interest in being an object of veneration, he used his personal popularity to cultivate attachment to the Union. He toured the entire country during his first term—an extraordinary feat before the development of turnpikes, railroads, and steamboats revolutionized transportation. He visited the New England states in the fall of 1789—carefully avoiding Rhode Island, which had not yet ratified the Constitution. He made a special trip to welcome Rhode Island into the Union in 1790. In April 1791 Washington set out on a tour of the South. He traveled through Richmond, Petersburg, and New Bern, North Carolina, on his way to Charleston, South Carolina. From there he moved on to Savannah, then west to Augusta, then north through the Carolina backcountry to Virginia, completing a journey of 1,887 miles in 67 days. Wherever he went, Washington met enthusiastic crowds and an outpouring of patriotic sentiment.

Washington also used these tours to cultivate respect for presidential authority. At a time when the sovereignty of the states was jealously defended, Washington refused to subordinate himself to state officials, even in their own states. When he visited Boston in the fall of 1789 Washington declined to make the first call on the governor, John Hancock. He insisted that Hancock come to him. Hancock claimed that he was suffering from gout, but Washington was unmoved. Hancock dutifully had himself carried into Washington's rented room on a stretcher.

Although he carefully husbanded the dignity of his office, Washington gave no reason to compare his tours to a traditional royal progress. He carefully maintained a plain, republic style of dress. His traveling parties were small, and did not include a military guard, although local militia officers occasionally insisted on escorting the president through their communities. Washington discouraged elaborate ceremonies, which interfered with his schedule, and scrupulously declined invitations to stay in private homes, preferring taverns and other public accommodations wherever they were available. By visiting every part of the new nation, Washington made the distant federal government— a tiny institution in a giant land—seem real to thousands of ordinary Americans. He assured them that the federal government was concerned with the needs of citizens in every part of the country and instilled in them a deeper attachment to the United States.

Establishing the dignity of the presidency without arousing anxieties about the executive power was difficult, but filling the many offices created by the new government presented Washington with as great a challenge. No responsibility laid before him so completely threatened his reputation for disinterested statesmanship. "I have no conception of a more delicate task than that which is imposed by the Constitution on the Executive," he wrote to a friend in March 1789: "It is the nature of Republicans, who are nearly in a state of equality, to be extremely jealous as to the disposal of all honorary or lucrative appointments." The political sensitivity of the problem was compounded by the number of applications he received from every part of the Union.

To all of these importunities, Washington responded in the same way: that he would go into public office "without being under any possible engagements of any nature whatsoever," and "would not be in the remotest degree influenced, in making nominations, by motives arising from ties of amity or blood, and that, on the other hand, three things ought to be regarded . . . the fitness of characters to fill offices, the comparative claims from the former merits & sufferings in service of the different Candidates, and the distribution of appointments in as equal a proportion as might be to persons belonging to the different States in the Union." Any other course, Washington felt certain, would expose the administration to "endless jealousies," and possibly "fatal consequences."[13]

Despite his misgivings, Washington was probably better suited to this task than any president since. He had no political debts to pay, and his family and friends, with a few minor exceptions, had no political ambitions to satisfy. He was a superb judge of character and talent. The range of his acquaintance, as a result of his service at the head of the Continental Army, was wider than that of any of his contemporaries. The American Revolution had produced an extraordinary generation of gifted men, and Washington knew most of them. He had seen, moreover, how many of these men behaved under pressure, in circumstances that revealed their fundamental natures.

By the fall of 1789 he had appointed some 125 officials. Except members of Congress, almost every federal official owed his place to Washington. He chose the heads of departments, Supreme Court justices, territorial governors and officials, ministers and consuls at foreign posts, Indian commissioners and superintendents, treasury officers, loan commissioners, customs officials, revenue officers, marshals, district attorneys, and federal court judges. He approved the appointment of army officers of every grade, Indian agents, and even lighthouse keepers. During eight years in office, Washington made nearly 400 nominations to office requiring Senate confirmation, and many other appointments left solely to his discretion. Filling such posts probably consumed more of Washington's time during the first year of his presidency than any other task.[14]

Washington's main criterion in making appointments was what he termed "fitness." For Washington, "fitness" did not refer primarily to technical ability, although ability to perform the duties of office was an important consideration. "Fitness" was mainly a judgment of character. A fit candidate for office was a man of unimpeachable personal integrity and bearing—sober, discreet, and reliable—and one well-regarded in his community or state. Washington's standard of "fitness" was not the impersonal standard generally applied to civil servants in modern times. It was the standard of a pre-modern, face-to-face society. It was implicitly elitist, since only gentlemen, in the pre-modern sense of that term, could possibly possess the kind of public reputation for integrity and public virtue that Washington demanded.

It is easy today to overlook the extraordinary importance—indeed the revolutionary implications—of this commitment on Washington's part. It now seems self-evident that appointed officials should be qualified in some meaningful sense for the offices they hold. But throughout the Western World in the eighteenth century, appointive posts were generally and frankly regarded as personal patronage to be dispensed at the pleasure of the appointing official. Many offices in the British and French administrative systems, particularly in the revenue services, were regarded as aristocratic sinecures, with office-holders receiving the fees and other emoluments of their positions while leaving the actual work to hired subordinates. Administrative reformers were beginning to remedy this situation in Britain and France during the 1780s, but their efforts were halting and uneven. Washington's standard—despite its pre-modern characteristics—was more advanced than that being applied in any contemporary government.

Some of his closest supporters and advisers, including Alexander Hamilton, expected Washington to use the patronage at his disposal to build a reliable group of administration allies in Congress—tying members of Congress to the President by lines of dependence and patronage by dispensing offices to the relatives of members and to their political allies in the states. Many members of Congress shared this expectation, and were among the first to importune Washington for patronage. But beyond requiring his nominees to be supporters of the Federal Constitution, Washington resisted the temptation to use the appointive power for political purposes. He looked beyond the immediate problem of building support in Congress to the greater problem of establishing the new government's reputation for rectitude. "No man," John Adams wrote in the summer of 1789, "I believe, has influence with the President. He seeks information from all quarters, and judges more independently than any man I ever knew."[15]

Washington's most important appointments were the heads of the three executive departments—war, treasury, and state. Henry Knox, Washington's former chief of artillery, had served at the head of the war department under the Confederation government, and Washington was happy to retain him in office. For the Treasury, Washington turned to Alexander Hamilton, one of his most able wartime aides-de-camp. For Secretary of State, Washington's choice fell on Thomas Jefferson, then serving as United States minister to France.

Washington sought to balance these and other appointments to high federal posts among the sections. Knox (along with Vice President John Adams) was from Massachusetts. Hamilton and Chief Justice John Jay were New Yorkers. Jefferson and Attorney General Edmund Randolph were Virginians. Early in the Washington presidency Pennsylvanians and South Carolinians grumbled that they received less than their share of prominent places in the executive and judicial branches, but Washington later appointed men from those states to major posts.[16]

Washington regarded Senate confirmation as a constitutional formality, and was dismayed when senators asserted their right to judge his nominees for themselves. In August 1789 the Senate rejected Benjamin Fishbourn as revenue officer of Savannah on the advice of Georgia Senator James Gunn. According to an account by the son of Washington's secretary Tobias Lear, "the President immediately repaired to the Senate Chambers & entered, to the astonishment of every one. The Vice-President left his chair & offered it to the President, who accepted it & then told the Senate that he had come to ask their reasons for rejecting his nomination." After an embarrassing silence, Gunn rose and explained that "his personal respect for the personal character of Genl. Washington was such that he would inform him of his grounds for recommending this rejection," but after doing so Gunn insisted that no explanation of the "motives or proceedings was ever due or would ever be given to any President of the United States." At that, Washington withdrew. The next day he addressed a letter to the Senate defending the nomination and insisting on Fishbourn's eminent fitness for office. The informal practice known as "senatorial courtesy," by which senators are acknowledged to have an informal veto power over federal appointments in their states, had its genesis in this incident. But this was a principle Washington never acknowledged.[17]

Fishbourn was only the first of Washington's nominees to be challenged by the Senate. In the Second Congress Senators began to challenge far more important nominations, including that of Anthony Wayne to serve as commander of the American army on the northwest frontier and Gouverneur Morris as minister to France. Later, in the intensely partisan atmosphere of the Jay Treaty debate, the Senate rejected Washington's nomination of John Rutledge as chief justice. Washington's unwavering appeal to an impartial standard of "fitness" for appointive office was nonetheless one of the most astute policies of his presidency, lifting the most potentially controversial power delegated to him above partisanship and insulating him from the charge that he was using presidential patronage to dominate the government.

At the outset, many people expected either the Secretary of State or the Secretary of the Treasury to act as a prime minister, leading the administration and shaping public policy while the President functioned as ceremonial head of the government. But Washington chose to be his own prime minister, and regarded his department heads as his subordinates. Their job, Washington explained to a French diplomat in 1789, was "to assist the supreme Magistrate in discharging the duties of his trust." In practice, Washington made all of the major decisions on foreign policy and the military—the areas in which he was most competent—and left the management of public finance to Hamilton.[18]

In his First Inaugural Address, Washington confessed that he was "unpracticed in the duties of civil administration," but in fact he was one of the most able administrators ever to serve as President. The experience of command in two wars and the cares of a great estate had taught him the value of systematic, orderly, and efficient daily management, which he demanded of his subordinates as well as himself. "System," he explained, "to all things is the soul of business. To deliberate maturely, and execute promptly is the way to conduct it to advantage." Washington was careful to ascertain facts before acting, but he acted promptly, with decisiveness and determination. He weighed the opinions of others, but relied ultimately on his own judgment and took full responsibility for actions undertaken on his instructions. He demanded the same systematic, responsible, and energetic conduct from his subordinates. He instructed his department heads "to deliberate maturely, but to execute promptly and vigorously. And not to put things off until the Morrow which can be done, and require to be done to day. Without an adherence to these rules, business will never be well done, or done in an easy manner; but will always be in arrear, with one thing treading upon the heels of another."[19]

Throughout his presidency, Washington maintained close control of his administration through a well-regulated system of consultation with his department heads. He typically referred official correspondence to the appropriate department. "If an answer was requisite," Thomas Jefferson later explained to his own presidential cabinet, "the Secretary of department communicated the letter & his proposed answer to the President. Generally they were simply sent back, after perusal, which signified his approbation. Sometimes he returned them with an informal note, suggesting an alteration or a query. If a doubt of any importance arose, he reserved it for conference. By this means he was always in accurate possession of all facts & proceedings in every part of the Union, & to whatsoever department they related; he formed a central point for the different branches, preserved an unity of object and action among them, exercised that participation in the gestion of affairs which his office made incumbent on him, and met himself the due responsibility for whatever was done."[20]

Washington's relationship with Congress reflected the same determination to make the presidency an energetic and effective institution, but was marked by greater caution and circumspection than any other aspect of his administration. Ideological hostility to executive power was based largely on the fear that a strong executive would corrupt and overawe the legislature and usurp its authority. Many of the powers of the presidency—including the direction of military and foreign affairs—had been carved out of the authority possessed by Congress under the Articles of Confederation. Legislation enacted by the First Congress granted the president extensive power over the executive departments, but many members of Congress remained understandably skeptical about the energetic use of presidential power and jealous of their prerogatives. Washington overcame these anxieties by scrupulously avoiding encroaching on those prerogatives. His main task, he insisted, was to execute the laws passed by Congress, not to devise a legislative program or interfere in the legislative process. The

"Constitution of the United States, & the Laws made under it" Washington explained to Edmund Randolph, "must mark the line of my official conduct."[21]

Although the Federal Constitution authorized the president to recommend suitable objects for legislation, Washington did so sparingly. Before Washington left Mount Vernon, his secretary David Humphreys prepared a draft inaugural address that made dozens of legislative proposals. Though it probably reflected ideas the two had discussed, Washington discarded the draft. In his First Inaugural Address Washington made only one specific legislative recommendation—that Congress consider amending the Constitution to safeguard individual rights against federal encroachment. Washington later used his annual messages to draw the attention of Congress to specific problems requiring legislative action. By using this authority sparingly, Washington ensured that his recommendations would be treated with greater respect.

Washington was even more circumspect in his use of the veto power—he used it just twice—but each instance was calculated to set a precedent defining the extent of presidential authority. The first time, in 1792, he vetoed a bill relating to the apportionment of congressional districts on the grounds that it was unconstitutional. Though the decision faced minor criticism, few people charged that Washington had exceeded his authority. Washington's second veto came just four days before he left office. The bill at issue included a provision calling for disbanding two dragoon companies. Washington vetoed the bill, explaining in his veto message that army needed the dragoons. Justifying his veto on grounds of policy, Washington set himself at odds with critics who argued that the veto could be justified only on the grounds of unconstitutionality. The House of Representatives attempted to override the veto, but when this effort failed Congress passed the original bill with the offending provision removed. Washington signed the new bill on his final day in office.

Washington's habits of deference toward Congress reassured Americans that a strong executive was not a threat to legislative independence. But Washington's deference also defined the line between congressional and presidential authority—a line he defended with determination when he believed Congress encroached on the prerogatives of the president. Washington construed presidential authority over military and foreign affairs broadly, and resisted congressional efforts to dictate in these areas. When the House of

Representatives threatened to intervene in the conduct of foreign relations by using the power of the purse to control the placement and grade of American diplomats abroad, Washington met privately with key senators and obtained changes to the bill that made it acceptable to him. Later Senate opponents of sending a minister to France tried to use the Senate's power to pass on presidential appointments to prevent Washington from sending a mission of any kind to Paris. Supporters of the administration again prevailed, preventing an open breach between Washington and the Senate. In early 1796 Washington refused a demand from the House of Representatives to turn over papers relating to John Jay's mission to Britain, on the grounds that the House had no authority over the conduct of foreign relations.

Washington was determined to defend the prerogatives of the president because he knew that precedents were being set that would shape the course of the American republic for generations. "Many things which appear of little importance of themselves and at the beginning," he wrote in May 1789, "may have great and durable consequences from their having been established at the commencement of a new general Government." He added wisely that it would be easier to begin with "a well adjusted system . . . than to correct errors or alter inconveniences after they shall have been confirmed by habit."[22]

Shortly after assuming the presidency, Washington wrote to his friend David Stuart that "the eyes of America—perhaps of the world—are turned to this Government; and many are watching the movements of all those who are concerned in its administration." Toward the end of his administration, Washington could write truthfully that the "powers of the Executive of the U. States are more definite, and better understood perhaps than those of almost any other Country; and my aim has been, and will continue to be, neither to stretch, nor relax from them in any instance whatever, unless imperious circumstances should render the measure indispensable." By working constantly to define the boundaries of presidential power, and scrupulously remaining within those boundaries, Washington proved himself an executive leader of considerable vision, integrity, and ability, while demonstrating to his countrymen that an energetic executive was not incompatible with republican liberty. In the process he conferred a dignity on the presidency that has made it possible for the institution to weather the conduct of his least admirable successors, and established precedents that have guided them all.[23]

CHAPTER TWO
A VISION OF PROSPERITY

WHEN GEORGE WASHINGTON ASSUMED THE PRESIDENCY, the United States government was mired in the greatest financial crisis in its history. The federal government began its life over $50 million in debt, more than thirty times what federal officials could expect to collect in taxes in a year. Most of this was the outstanding Revolutionary War debts of the Continental Congress. About $11 million was owed to the French government and Dutch bankers and about $40 million was owed on various debt instruments held by citizens of the United States. These included certificates for money loaned for the cause, food and supplies confiscated for the army, and back pay for soldiers. The Confederation government had never had a dependable source of revenue with which to service these debts. At the end of its life the Confederation was nearing bankruptcy, its securities propped up by occasional infusions of capital from Dutch creditors, who had sunk so much into the American government that they were unwilling to allow their investment to become utterly worthless. Most holders of the domestic debt were convinced that they would never be paid in full. Prior to the constitutional convention all forms of government debt traded at a fraction of face value, in some cases less than ten percent. The ratification of the Federal Constitution boosted investor confidence and pushed the price of government securities higher, but most of the domestic debt was still circulating at a fraction of its face value when Washington took office.

Washington understood that the economic future of the United States depended upon successfully resolving the debt crisis and establishing the new nation's finances on a sound basis. Unless adequate provision was made for the debt, the public credit would be ruined. The United States would lack the means to conduct its affairs, and would sink back into weakness and insignificance. Washington's wartime

Washington's Treading Barn. Washington's sixteen-sided treading barn reflected the same passion for rational improvement that characterized his vision of the American economy.

21

experience had taught him the importance of ensuring the government possessed adequate financial resources. The Revolutionary War had been protracted needlessly, Washington believed, because Congress had been unwilling and unable to command sufficient resources to bring it to a swift conclusion. Washington found this particularly frustrating, because he was certain that the United States was a nation of almost limitless economic potential—with a rapidly growing population, enormous natural resources, a seemingly inexhaustible expanse of undeveloped land, and an extensive network of navigable rivers to facilitate commerce. Measured against the potential of the American economy, Washington did not believe that the national debt was unmanageably large. He seems, in fact, to have been unrealistically optimistic about discharging it quickly without imposing a large tax burden on the American people.

Resolving the debt crisis by creating a financial system that would harness the productive capacity of the American economy to the needs of the federal government was one of the most important accomplishments of the Washington presidency. But it was not primarily Washington's accomplishment. The initial impetus came from Congress, which began considering a revenue system in the spring of 1789. Congress quickly decided to seek recommendations on the more complicated problem of financing the debt from the Secretary of the Treasury. The technical aspects of public finance—the intricacies of taxation, debt service, and commercial regulation—were alien to Washington, as they were to most of his contemporaries. Washington's role was to appoint someone to the treasury who could devise a financial program that would win the support of Congress, and to ensure that the program was administered with a thoroughness and impartiality that would minimize sectional tensions and command respect from every part of the Union.

As soon as Congress passed legislation organizing the Department of the Treasury, Washington named Alexander Hamilton as its first secretary. Hamilton served as one of Washington's aides-de-camp during the Revolutionary War, and his extraordinary administrative ability led Washington to delegate a wide array of responsibilities to him. Given a field command just before the siege of Yorktown, he distinguished himself for bravery in an attack on the British lines. After leaving the army Hamilton was admitted to the New York bar (after a few months of intensive study), and served as a delegate to the Confederation Congress, where his grasp of public finance was readily apparent. He was a member of the constitutional convention in 1787 and was the principal author of *The Federalist,* already recognized as the most thorough exposition of the Federal Constitution. Hamilton was closely identified with Robert Morris and his circle, an important group of Federalist merchants, financiers, lawyers and politicians. His appointment was greeted with approval from most of the financial community. He was just thirty-two years old—the youngest person ever named to a cabinet-level post in American history. Handsome, charming, and possessed of a penetrating intelligence, a passion for order, and enormous energy, Hamilton became Washington's most trusted subordinate.

Hamilton possessed the genius to master almost any administrative problem, but his ability to make difficult matters seem simple (even when he had devoted hard study to them) made many men distrust him. This distrust was compounded by his combative nature and an unwillingness to suffer fools gladly, particularly unfortunate character-istics for an officer whose work involved government activities—including taxation and the payment of the national debt—that would touch the lives of nearly everyone in the country. Proud, self-assured, and impatient, he made enemies too easily. Hamilton was also ambitious for fame and extremely sensitive about his honor. Washington was all too aware of these characteristics, since they had prompted Hamilton's resignation from his military staff in 1781. But Washington believed that Hamilton's noblest aspirations—above all Hamilton's thirst for fame—would be enough to keep his less admirable tendencies in check, at least until he had completed the work of reorganizing and rationalizing the nation's finances.

It was a gargantuan task. In addition to the more than $50 million the federal government owed to its creditors, the individual states still owed approximately $25 million in outstanding war debts. The federal government was not obliged to pay state debts, but since Hamilton intended the federal government to take over sources of revenue available to the debtor states it would be good policy, he believed, for the federal government to assume responsibility for state debts as well. Together, the foreign, domestic, and state debts bore an annual interest (at rates ranging from four to six percent) of about $4.5 million. This interest alone was about three times what the federal treasury could expect to collect through customs duties, which were the first taxes levied by the new Congress and which would be the main source of federal revenue at Hamilton's disposal. In short, it seemed almost

New York's Federal Hall, seen here in a contemporary engraving of Washington's inauguration, was the scene of congressional debates over Alexander Hamilton's proposals to fund the public debt.

impossible to imagine how the United States was going to keep up with the interest on its debts, much less repay any of the principal.

Various solutions to the financial crisis had been proposed before Hamilton took office. Most involved some form of debt repudiation. One suggestion was to scale the principal on all but the foreign debt back to the prevailing market price. A more popular suggestion involved discriminating between original holders of the Continental debt, who would be paid the face value of their securities, and subsequent holders, mostly speculators, who would receive the market price for their certificates, while the balance could be paid to the original holders. This modified form of repudiation, which seemed to do justice to soldiers and farmers forced to accept Continental securities in lieu of pay, was championed by James Madison. Washington probably sympathized with this idea. He regretted sending soldiers home at the end of the Revolutionary War with certificates of debt instead of pay, knowing that financial necessity would compel them to sell the certificates to "unfeeling, avaricious speculators" for a fraction of their face value. But Washington probably understood that the idea was impractical. Discriminating between original holders and subsequent buyers would have demolished public credit by effectively making all government securities non-negotiable; investors would never buy securities they could not securely trade. Washington acknowledged that Madison's defense of the idea was prompted "by the purest motives," but concluded that it "had better never been stirred." Some of the most prominent moneyed men were demanding prompt payment in full at face value, something the federal government simply could not raise sufficient money to accomplish.[24]

Hamilton rejected all of these suggestions. What he proposed was to monetize the debt. He had no illusions about retiring it quickly. His "Report on Public Credit," presented to the House of Representatives in January 1790, urged Congress to devote a regular source of revenue to paying the annual interest on the debt. Unlike annual appropriations that had the appearance of stopgap measures, this would stabilize the value of debt instruments and make it possible for them to circulate like money. This would help solve one of the endemic problems of the United States: the constant shortage of a stable medium of exchange. Hamilton justifiably expected that an increase in the money supply would stimulate the economy and lead to an increase in federal revenues, but he did not rest his plan to fund the debt on that foundation.

First, he proposed to renegotiate the interest rate down to a uniform four percent by opening a new loan, to which holders of the domestic debt could subscribe by presenting their existing securities. Only this portion of the domestic debt would be funded, which would encourage holders of securities drawing more than four percent to subscribe to the new loan. Even with the interest on the domestic debt reduced to four percent, federal revenues would not be sufficient to fund it. Hamilton consequently proposed to raise customs duties on imported tea, coffee, and spirits. At the end of 1790, he proposed an additional excise tax on domestically distilled spirits. Excise taxes were extremely unpopular with the American people. It was the excise on tea that had led to the Boston Tea Party in 1774. Hamilton was not anxious to excite popular unrest, but he could not see any palatable alternative to an excise. Congress passed the Excise Act at the beginning of 1791. The tax made nearly everyone in the federal government nervous. Washington set off on his tour of the southern states a few weeks after the excise was adopted, and everywhere he went he made inquiries about how the new tax law was being received.

Hamilton borrowed the crucial feature of his financial system, the "sinking fund," from British practice, but intended it for a new purpose. In Britain, the sinking fund received specific excess revenues and used them to enter the securities market and retire the principal on the debt. Hamilton's fund was to work in the same way, receiving excess revenues from the postal service and other sources and using them to retire federal securities. But Hamilton also intended to use the fund to enter the market to drive up the value of the federal debt whenever it fluctuated downward, serving a function similar to that of the modern Federal Reserve. To provide the federal treasury with a reliable institutional connection to financial markets, Hamilton proposed that Congress grant a charter to a Bank of the United States, which would hold federal deposits, issue paper money, and provide the federal government and the commercial community with banking services. Because of its similarity to the Bank of England, and because its commercial operations would disproportionately benefit northern merchants, this proved to be one of the most controversial elements of the program.

Hamilton's program was intended to accomplish much more than just resolve the nation's debt crisis. Hamilton aimed to establish the conditions necessary for the United States to realize its enormous economic potential. He believed that this potential was being stifled by oligarchic control and other social conventions that discouraged innovation by failing to reward industry. Hamilton was not, however, an economic liberal. Though he was committed to a market economy and private enterprise, Hamilton rejected a central premise of liberal economic doctrine—that if governments did not interfere in the economy, market forces would direct human industry to the most useful, efficient, and productive employment, as if guided by an invisible hand. "Experience teaches," Hamilton wrote, "that men are often so much governed by what they are accustomed to see and practice, that the simplest and most obvious improvements, in the most ordinary occupations, are adopted with hesitation, reluctance, and slow gradations." The natural order, Hamilton believed, was for social conventions, habits, and values to dictate economic patterns. Government action typically reflected these norms. Hamilton, as his biographer Forrest McDonald explains, "saw the advantages of turning the formula around, of using government to bring about economic changes which in turn would alter society for its own benefit." Hamilton aimed to facilitate the development of a competitive society that rewarded industry and skill, and in which money, rather than tradition or inherited social standing, would be the ultimate arbiter of worth. In the process the United States would become a powerful commercial republic, its people energetic, prosperous and free.[25]

Hamilton's plan was brilliant, but it was difficult for ordinary citizens to understand and it engendered little enthusiasm among them. Its revolutionary social implications were opaque. National in design, it gave the appearance of favoring the interests of the North over those of the South and West, and speculators over everyone else. Forcing up the value of almost-worthless Continental securities would set off a speculative frenzy that would, indeed, benefit men who had liquid capital to invest, almost all of whom were northern merchants. Hamilton reasoned that this onetime windfall for speculators was an acceptable trade-off for establishing American credit, but he did not anticipate how deeply the speculative frenzy would alienate southerners. Citizens of the southern states (except South Carolina, which still owed a considerable war debt and thus benefited by assumption) saw Hamilton's financial program as a device to burden them with taxes to enrich northern speculators.

A more serious problem with Hamilton's financial program was that it tied the nation's fiscal security to British commerce. Hamilton's scheme depended on the steady collection of tariff revenues on imports. These were inevitably British imports. After the Revolutionary War, British merchants had resumed their accustomed business of supplying manufactured goods to the American market and taking away American grain and other commodities in trade. American merchants were used to this pattern. No other nation was prepared to take Britain's place as a trading partner. When Washington assumed the presidency, 90 percent of American imports came from Britain. Hamilton was prepared to go to great lengths not to antagonize the British, and opposed any policy that might disrupt Anglo-American trade.

Hamilton presented his program in stages, through a series of reports laid before Congress between 1790 and 1792. Each of the provisions—funding and assumption, tariff revisions, the federal excise, and the Bank of the United States—were fiercely contested. Hamilton's program was opposed by congressman from every part of the United States, but the most unreserved critics came from Washington's Virginia, where British commercial and fiscal arrangements were regarded with particular abhorrence. Much of the Virginia gentry was in more or less perpetual debt to British merchants, and had looked to American independence to break their dependence on British credit. A financial program that tied the nation's economy to British trade was hateful to them. Congressional opposition was led by James Madison, who had been Washington's most important adviser in the first months of the administration. Hamilton's supporters came mainly from New England and the Middle States and were led by Fisher Ames in the House and Robert Morris in the Senate. These supporters secured the adoption of most of Hamilton's proposals. Congress insisted on minor changes (the domestic debt was refinanced at three different interest rates, for example, rather than a uniform four percent), and took no action at all on Hamilton's final report, presented in 1792, which called for an elaborate effort to encourage manufacturing.

Washington had nothing to do with devising Hamilton's program and did not campaign openly for its adoption, since that would have been regarded as executive encroachment on the prerogatives of the legislature. It also would have exposed Washington to the charge of favoring the interests of the commercial classes of the North over those of the planters and small farmers of the South and West, compromising his reputation for equanimity and disinterested leadership in precisely those parts of the country where his moral authority would be most needed to buttress the program once it was passed. Washington husbanded his political capital with great care, and was an astute judge of when to expend it for maximum effect. Though he did not play a part in formulating the administration's financial program or an active role securing its passage, his silence preserved the reputation for impartial statesmanship that enabled him to secure compliance with the law and rebuff its most serious critics. Washington's silence while Hamilton's proposals were being debated in Congress was nonetheless regarded as tacit approval of the measures recommended by the treasury secretary. The few guarded comments Washington made in his private correspondence about Hamilton's proposals validate this assumption.[26]

Washington approved of Hamilton's program because the two men had similar visions of the United States as a powerful, prosperous commercial republic. Washington did not understand the sophisticated mechanics of the plan, but he was persuaded that it would restore the national credit that he knew was essential to the preservation of the Union. Like Hamilton, Washington regarded the United States as a nation of almost limitless commercial potential. He had no doubt that Americans had the means to develop this potential, but he worried that they would fail to recognize the opportunity. Like Hamilton, he was frustrated by the extent to which tradition and convention seemed to stifle economic innovation and improvement. He marveled that "Providence has dealt her favors to us with so profuse a hand," and prayed that his countrymen "may have wisdom enough to improve them."[27]

The American Revolution was shaped by a widespread anxiety about the emergence of commercial society. The Revolutionary generation witnessed an extraordinary surge in commercial development, particularly in the retail consumption of imported British manufactures—lace tablecloths and Staffordshire china, fine fabrics and metal buttons, and a broad array of other goods that had once been available only to the wealthy. This American consumer revolution paralleled similar developments in Britain a generation earlier. Many American revolutionaries feared that the development of a consumer oriented commercial order in the United States would lead to the kind of social degeneration and political corruption that they associated with Britain. Consumer society, they argued, robbed men of personal independence by seducing them to live beyond their means, entangling them in a web of debt, and creating a large class of manufacturing wage-laborers dependent on employers. They also contended that commercialization encouraged people to focus their energy on private gain and to disregard the broader interests of society.[28]

Washington was influenced by this ideological preoccupation with the enervating effects of a consumer-oriented commercial order. In 1783 he confessed to Thomas Jefferson that commerce "has its advantages and disadvantages," and that among the latter were "those vices which luxury, the consequence of wealth and power, naturally introduce." But his misgivings about luxury were insignificant compared with his enthusiasm for American commerce. He did not believe that the pursuit of commercial gain was inconsistent with the broader interests of society. "A people," he wrote in 1784, "who are possessed of the spirit of Commerce—who see, & who will pursue their advantages, may achieve almost anything."[29]

Washington believed that commerce was an agent of refinement rather than corruption. When he reflected "on the probable influence that commerce may here after have on human manners & society in general," Washington concluded that the "fraternal ties" of commerce were making individuals "less barbarous" and nations "more humanized in their policy." In a commercial society, a taste for finer things stimulated industry and inventiveness. The "spirit of Commerce" Washington praised was characterized by a passion for economic improvement through long-term, rational investment, was motivated by benevolence rather than avarice and looked beyond the short-term gains pursued by speculators.[30]

Washington found the "spirit of Commerce" most fully developed in the economically sophisticated Middle States. Washington spent a considerable amount of time in this region during and after the Revolutionary War and he identified closely with city-dwellers like Robert Morris and John Jay. He embraced their refined tastes. He enjoyed the theater, museums, and other urban amusements. He found the people of the Middle States more enterprising, industrious, and efficient than southerners. He found their schools better and their agriculture more rational. He admired their inventiveness, was excited by their spirit of experimentation, and delighted in their passion for economic improvements. He sought out their latest labor-saving machines to try at Mount Vernon.[31]

Mount Vernon, indeed, was a monument to Washington's passion for rational improvement. Washington posed as a simple farmer who wanted nothing more than to retire "beneath my own vine and fig tree," but Mount Vernon was much more than a farm. It was a complicated commercial enterprise, combining staple crop agriculture, domestic manufacturing, a commercial fishery, and a mill—complete with labor-saving machinery designed by Oliver Evans, the leading millwright in the Middle States, whose inventions were vital to the American Industrial Revolution. Washington's crop experiments, mule breeding, his preference for ditching and hedging over impermanent rail fences, his demand that his managers make detailed reports on the disposition of Mount Vernon's labor force, and his fascination with the latest agricultural innovations—like his sixteen-sided treading barn—were all reflections of his improving spirit. So was his increasing frustration with slavery as a labor system.

Washington's passion for improvement was most fully expressed in his efforts to improve the navigation of the Potomac River. He was convinced that developing inland navigation was the key to unleashing the economic potential of the United States, and he believed that the Potomac, which penetrates far into the Appalachian barrier, offered the most practical water route between the Atlantic coast and the Ohio Valley. After the Revolutionary War, Washington became the president of the Potomac Company, which received a charter from Virginia and Maryland to improve the navigation of the river by removing rocks from the channel and building canals around the falls, with the long-term goal of opening the Potomac to trans-Appalachian commerce by way of a portage linking a tributary of the Potomac in western Pennsylvania to the Ohio River system.

Washington's confidence that commercial intercourse would soon be opened between the Ohio country and the Atlantic market led him to differ with Hamilton about the relative importance of manufacturing and agriculture for American prosperity. Washington's economic ideas were influenced by the mercantilist conception of national wealth. Mercantilists imagined that the world's wealth was fixed, and that one nation's gain was another's loss, making national prosperity dependant on a favorable balance of trade. Mercantilist theory dictated that a nation seek to maximize the value of exports and minimize that of imports, which would ensure the nation an increasing share of the world's wealth. Mercantilists attached little importance to the domestic marketplace—which seemed to them to be nothing more than shuffling money from one hand to another without adding anything to the national wealth—except insofar as domestic production decreased dependence on imports.

Since Americans consumed large amounts of British manufactured goods, Washington believed that it was in the interest of the United States to free itself from dependence on imports by stimulating domestic manufacturing. But he did not believe that American manufactures would compete with British goods in foreign markets within the foreseeable future, so schemes to encourage manufacturing by high tariffs or government subsidies held little appeal for him. "I would not force the introduction of manufactures, by extravagant encouragements, and to the prejudice of agriculture" he wrote in 1789, "yet, I conceive, much might be done in that way by women, children & others; without taking one really necessary hand from tilling the earth."[32]

Washington looked instead to the expansion of commercial

agriculture as the basis for America's future prosperity. He expected that American settlers would quickly fill up the trans-Appalachian West and put millions of new acres in cultivation. Hamilton, by contrast, believed that the peopling of the trans-Appalachian West would take several decades. While expecting agriculture to retain its accustomed position as the principal occupation of the American people, he looked to manufacturing to improve the balance of trade, first by satisfying domestic demand, and later by making American manufactures a major export. Although nothing turned out quite the way either man expected, Washington anticipated the future of American trade more accurately than Hamilton. Neither man, however, appreciated the productive capacity of the domestic marketplace, which became the real basis of American economic strength.

Hamilton's financial system, administered with the passion for detail that was one of Hamilton's great strengths, proved to be an extraordinarily effective means for resolving the nation's debt crisis, securing the confidence of investors in the federal government, and stimulating economic activity. By 1792 most federal securities were trading at or near their face value, and the national debt was placed on the path to gradual extinction. When subscriptions were opened for shares in the Bank of the United States in the summer of 1791, the shares were all sold within hours—solid proof, Washington wrote, "of the confidence reposed in our measures." At the same time, the country experienced the first stages of a commercial boom, prompted in part by increased European demand for American commodities and a flight of European capital to the United States. Washington was not inclined to impute to Hamilton's system improvements in the economy that were "due only to the goodness of Providence." But by July 1791 he could report that "Our public credit stands on that ground which three years ago it would have been considered as a species of madness to have foretold."[33]

Despite its success—perhaps, in large measure, because of it— Hamilton's program was subjected to almost constant criticism. Much to Washington's disappointment, one of the most severe critics was his own Secretary of State. Thomas Jefferson possessed one of the most comprehensive intellects of the eighteenth century. Yet he was surprisingly obtuse about economics, which alternately bewildered and frustrated him. He was also prone, like many other Americans, to look anxiously for plots and conspiracies against liberty at work in government. He had no difficulty imagining such a conspiracy in the efforts of the Secretary of the Treasury to resolve the nation's debt crisis through a system that imitated the fiscal policies of Britain. Jefferson had a profound loathing for the British government, which he regarded as irredeemably corrupt. By the beginning of 1791 he came to regard Hamilton's financial system, the operation of which he never understood, as the leading edge of a conspiracy to subvert American liberty and erect a monarchy on its ruins.

Washington never took Jefferson's charges seriously, and rebuffed every effort Jefferson made to undermine his confidence in Hamilton. Whatever the demerits of Hamilton's financial system—and Washington assured Jefferson that he did not agree with every part of it—Washington never questioned Hamilton's motives or integrity. He was convinced, moreover, that maintaining the independence of the United States depended upon increasing the economic strength of the nation, and he was certain that commercial development was the only effective way of reaching that goal. He had no sympathy with the view that commercialization would corrupt the American people, undermine their personal independence and ultimately destroy the republic. He was certain that commerce would make the United States powerful and prosperous, and provide Americans with the means to protect their freedom.[34]

Thomas Jefferson and his political allies never relinquished the view that Hamilton's financial system was part of a conspiracy to subvert American liberty. But they could not believe that Washington was a part of that conspiracy. They concluded that he simply did not understand what Hamilton was up to, implying that Washington was a rustic simpleton duped into supporting the evil designs of the treasury secretary. Hamilton himself unwittingly contributed to this pernicious absurdity by describing Washington as "an aegis very essential to me." An "aegis" is a magical shield. But in the political struggle over his financial program, it was Hamilton who absorbed most of the blows. He was, in fact, Washington's shield—devising and pushing through Congress a brilliant fiscal plan that set the country on a path toward economic strength that Washington wanted the nation to follow. Hamilton's financial program made the treasury secretary one of the most controversial men in the United States. Its success ensured the economic future of the Union Washington worked so hard to secure.

CHAPTER THREE
A CONTINENTAL REPUBLIC

AT A TIME WHEN MOST MEN thought of their state as their "country," the sweep of Washington's national vision was startling in its magnificence. Washington envisioned a continental republic extending, not just along the Atlantic seaboard, but westward through the Ohio and Mississippi valleys. Once these lands were made secure for settlers and joined to the seaboard states by reliable avenues for commerce, Washington predicted, they would "settle faster than any other ever did, or any one would imagine."[35] One of the most important accomplishments of Washington's presidency was to secure the West for American settlers, making possible the extraordinary westward expansion of the American Union that occurred during the first decades of the nineteenth century.

When Washington assumed the presidency, American expansion into the West was blocked by the Indians living on the frontier and by Britain and Spain, whose possessions surrounded the new nation on three sides. In the Southwest, native tribes were struggling to slow American settlement in western Georgia and what would become the states of Kentucky, Tennessee, Alabama, and Mississippi. In the Old Northwest native tribes contested American settlement along the Ohio River and its tributaries.

To the north the British maintained their hold on Canada and retained a series of fortified posts on the American side of the Great Lakes, including forts at Oswego, Niagara, and Detroit. The British were to have surrendered these posts to the United States following the Revolutionary War, but they declined to do so until Americans fulfilled their obligation to pay pre-war debts owed British subjects. This was a mere pretext. The posts were a valuable link in the Canadian fur-trading network and were the basis of British influence with the Indian tribes of

George Washington's Globe. *The globe in Washington's Mount Vernon study is a reminder of his vision of the United States as a continental republic.*

the Ohio Valley.

Spanish territory bordered the United States on the west and south. The Spanish controlled East and West Florida, the lower Mississippi Valley, including the port of New Orleans, and the enormous trans-Mississippi province of Louisiana. This vast domain was sparsely peopled and lightly defended. To discourage American settlements that would threaten their hold on the region, the Spanish closed the lower Mississippi River to American commerce. This policy infuriated American settlers, but many of them were as angry at the American government for its apparent disinterest in reversing the policy as they were at the Spanish. To exploit this rising contempt for the United States government, the Spanish sent agents into Kentucky and Tennessee to encourage separation from the United States. Through these agents, the Spanish scattered bribes among southwestern leaders and hinted that the Mississippi would be opened to independent settlements allied with Spain.

Washington was not concerned that Britain or Spain would attempt to conquer the western territory of the United States. He worried that economic necessity would push American settlers toward their foreign neighbors. As long as the Mississippi River remained the cheapest way to get Ohio Valley produce to market, Washington realized, American settlers in Kentucky, Tennessee, and the Northwest Territory would form increasingly close ties to Spain. Eventually the western settlements might ally themselves with Spain or even accept Spanish rule in order to enjoy unrestricted access to the Mississippi. "The Western settlers," Washington wrote, "stand as it were upon a pivot—the touch of a feather would turn them any way."[36]

The Confederation government had engaged in years of futile diplomacy to persuade Britain to relinquish the posts and Spain to open the Mississippi to American commerce. Washington had no faith in these efforts. Washington did not believe the British would surrender their posts, nor the Spanish open the Mississippi, until the United States asserted its authority over the West by subduing the hostile Indians. The challenge before the federal government, as Washington saw it, was to maintain peace with the European powers, secure the western settlements by pacifying the hostile Indian tribes, and open regular commercial routes between East and West that would cement the trans-Appalachian settlements to the United States by bonds of economic interest. This would ensure the rapid peopling of the West by American settlers and compel Britain and Spain to grant concessions to the

United States.

Pacifying the West was the first challenge. Prior to the Revolution, the British had maintained peace with the western Indian tribes by forbidding settlement west of the Appalachians. During the Revolutionary War, the new American governments tried to prevent encroachment on Indian land—not because they respected Indian rights but because they were reluctant to embroil themselves in Indian wars. Settlers ignored their edicts and poured over the Appalachians into the valleys of Kentucky and Tennessee and into the upper Ohio Valley. Alarmed Indians allied themselves with the British and attacked American settlements all along the frontier. Congress and the states did little to assist the frontiersmen, fostering a spirit of independence and a distrust of central government that threatened to alienate the trans-Appalachian West from the new nation.

The warring tribes inflicted considerable losses on American settlers, and Indian warriors were surprised and angered when the British made peace with the United States without regard for their interests. Many warriors simply continued to fight. Britain and Spain, though officially at peace with the United States, secretly provided the hostile Indians with arms and ammunition, using the Indians as a surrogate army to combat American expansion. Lord Dorchester, the governor of Canada, believed the security of that colony depended on keeping the Indians between advancing American settlers and the Canadian frontier. The Spanish depended on the Indian tribes of the southern interior, particularly the Creeks and Cherokees, to resist the advance of American settlement. With a steady supply of arms, hostile warriors were able to keep constant pressure on the American frontier.

Probably no American was better prepared to deal with this situation than George Washington. He had engaged in his first Indian negotiations at age twenty-one, when the lieutenant governor of Virginia sent him to warn the French out of the upper Ohio Valley. His service with General Edward Braddock's ill-fated expedition to drive the French away from the forks of the Ohio, which met disaster in the Battle of the Monongahela in 1755, had taught him never to underestimate the ability of Indians to defeat an army once it passed the frontier. This lesson was lost on many of his contemporaries, who expected the Indians to run at the sight of a European-style army.

Washington had no affection for Indians. He respected their ability in woodland warfare but had none of the sentimental illusions about the "Noble Savage" common among genteel easterners who had no conception of the ugliness and brutality of frontier war. Washington was equally realistic about frontier settlers, whom he distrusted as much or more than he did Indians. Washington had been obliged to evict squatters from his western lands on several occasions and he regarded frontiersmen as a generally dishonest and shifty lot who were responsible for inciting the Indians to violence. "In vain we may expect peace with the Indians on our frontiers," Washington wrote, "so long as a lawless set of unprincipled wretches can violate the rights of hospitality, or infringe the most solemn treaties, without receiving the punishment they so justly merit."[37]

As president Washington sought to pacify the Indians, by negotiation when possible, by force when necessary, but always in a manner calculated to prevent the formation of a general Indian confederacy or the outbreak of a general Indian war. Such a war, Washington knew, would be a disaster for the new nation, draining the federal treasury, arousing traditional suspicions of standing armies, raising tensions between federal and state authorities, and exciting jealousy and disagreements between the states. A general Indian war on the frontier, Washington understood, would endanger the Union.

Washington first made peace with the Creeks, the most powerful and warlike tribe in the South. The Creeks occupied western Georgia, most of modern Alabama and part of Tennessee. Their most important leader was a shrewd negotiator named Alexander McGillivray. The son of a Scots trader and a half-Creek, half-French woman, McGillivray was educated in Charleston and later apprenticed to a merchant in Savannah. When his father returned to Scotland during the Revolutionary War, McGillivray joined the Indians. He was appointed the British agent to the Creeks and served British interests by dispatching war parties against American settlements. When the British surrendered West Florida to Spain at the end of the Revolutionary War, McGillivray forged an alliance with the Spanish and launched a war against the American settlements on the northern and eastern boundaries of the Creek territory.

The Creek war had been going on for nearly three years when Washington assumed the presidency. The Confederation government had tried, without success, to negotiate an end to the conflict. Washington was determined to succeed where the Confederation Congress had failed. A military campaign against the Creeks was not an option. Secretary of War Henry Knox estimated that it would take 2,800 men to subjugate the Creeks, at a time the entire federal military

Washington rented a mansion on Broadway in New York for his official residence. He recieved the visiting Creek chiefs there in July 1790.

establishment consisted of fewer than 700 men. In 1789 Washington dispatched a three-man commission to negotiate with McGillivray at Rock Landing on the Oconee River, but the Creek chief walked out when it became clear that the commissioners were not empowered to make substantial concessions. The exasperated commissioners urged Washington to raise an army to put down the Creeks.

Washington decided to give diplomacy another try. He employed Marinus Willett, who had distinguished himself fighting the Indians on the New York frontier, as a personal envoy. Willett persuaded McGillivray to travel to New York to meet with the President. When McGillivray and his party arrived, Washington treated them like visiting royalty. He received McGillivray repeatedly—and sought to keep the Creek leaders away from Spanish agents, who were armed with bribes and intent on breaking up the negotiations. On August 7, 1790, McGillivray and his chiefs signed the Treaty of New York, acknowledging American sovereignty over a portion of Creek territory and ceding a disputed strip of land on the Georgia border to that state. On behalf of the United States, Washington pledged to oppose land companies threatening to encroach on Creek land. Secret articles of the treaty appointed McGillivray United States agent to the Creeks, and granted him an annual payment of $1,500.

No one understood better than Washington that McGillivray was playing the United States against Spain in an effort to gain advantage over both. The alarmed Spanish soon renewed their pledges of support to the Creeks and increased their annual payment to McGillivray. Desultory fighting continued on the southwestern frontier after a pause that lasted just a few months. But Washington justly regarded the treaty as a success, and described it is as the "main foundation of the future peace and prosperity of the South Western frontier of the United States." The treaty also dramatically raised the prestige of the federal government by demonstrating that the Washington administration was capable of resolving a frontier conflict that had frustrated the best efforts of the Confederation. The Creek treaty was followed in 1791 by a treaty with the Cherokees. Savage fighting with the Creeks and Cherokees erupted several times during the remainder of Washington's presidency, but the administration managed to prevent a general Indian war in the southwest.[38]

Pacifying the Ohio frontier proved more difficult. Though the governor of the Northwest Territory, Arthur St. Clair, concluded a treaty a few months before Washington assumed the presidency, no important chiefs signed the agreement and few warriors were prepared to abide by its terms. Warriors of the Miami, Shawnee, Wabash, and other tribes continued to resist the westward push of settlement down the Ohio River into the Northwest Territory, and raided frontier settlements and killed scores of people in 1789 and early 1790. Washington, Knox, and St. Clair decided to conduct a punitive expedition against these tribes, not just to stop them from attacking settlers but to discourage other Indians from joining them.

In September 1790 a mixed force of 1,453 men—320 regulars and 1,133 militia—under the command of Brigadier General Josiah Harmar marched northward from Fort Washington, which guarded the American settlement at Cincinnati. Their aim was to capture and destroy Kekionga, known to Americans as the Miami Village. Located where the Saint Marys and Saint Joseph rivers meet to form the Maumee (the site of modern Fort Wayne, Indiana), Kekionga was the most important of several Indian towns in the vicinity and a center for trade with the British. Harmar expected the Indians to give battle to defend Kekionga, but as his army approached, they set fire to the village and fled. Emboldened by the apparent ease of his victory, Harmar permitted a detachment to march on a nearby village on the Eel River. Before the Americans reached the village, Indian warriors led by Miami chief Little

Turtle ambushed them. They killed most of the thirty regulars and the few militiamen who stood and fought. The rest of the detachment fled in disorder back to Harmar's camp, setting off a panic among the remaining militia. After destroying other villages in the vicinity, Harmar decided to retreat to Fort Washington. But as he began his retreat he sent another detachment to attack Indian warriors returning to Kekionga. This detachment was also routed with heavy losses. Harmar's men then retreated in disorder back to the Ohio.

Harmar reported that the raid was a success, but Washington and Knox, along with most congressmen, regarded it as a disaster. Washington blamed the fiasco on Harmar, but it seems to have been due as much to haste, poor planning, and heavy reliance on the militia. Whatever the cause of the failure, the consequences were evident almost immediately. Indian warriors—enraged by the looting and destruction of their villages and emboldened by the victories over Harmar's detachments—raided frontier communities along the upper Ohio and attacked outlying settlements in Pennsylvania, Virginia, and Kentucky. State officials pressed for a response and threatened to take military action on their own if none was forthcoming from the federal government. In western New York, unrest spread to the chiefs of the Six Nations and it seemed possible that their warriors would join the hostile tribes. The failure of Harmar's expedition broadened the Indian conflict and threatened to erode the military authority of the federal government.

Washington decided to a send a new expedition to occupy the heart of the Indian country and establish a permanent fort at Kekionga. He put the expedition under the command of the territorial governor, Arthur St. Clair, who received a commission as a major general, his former rank in the Continental Army. To provide St. Clair with sufficient men, the administration asked Congress to double the size of the army and to authorize the war department to organize temporary levies in the nearby states. The proposal aroused old anxieties about standing armies, but the magnitude of the problem overwhelmed these concerns. Congress approved the expansion of the army and appropriated funds to finance St. Clair's expedition, which was expected to set out in the summer. Washington cautioned St. Clair to guard against an ambush.

St. Clair's army of some 2,600 men marched from a post north of Fort Washington in September 1791, several weeks later than expected. The troops constructed a fort on the Great Miami River and pressed north toward the Maumee, halting to construct a second fort a few miles south of present Greenville, Ohio. The weather, which had been unseasonably fair, turned wet and cold in mid-October. Clothing and tents intended for a summer campaign afforded little protection from the freezing rain; shoddy uniforms provided by unscrupulous contractors fell apart; thousands of musket cartridges were spoiled, and rations began to run out. Daily desertions forced St. Clair to impose harsh discipline to keep his army from disintegrating. But he pushed north.

On November 3, the army—reduced by detachments and desertions to about 1,400 men—camped near the Wabash River. The next morning warriors under the command of Little Turtle attacked the camp and delivered one of the most crushing defeats ever suffered by the United States Army at the hands of the Indians. The dead included St. Clair's second-in-command, General Richard Butler, who was mortally wounded and abandoned on the battlefield. The panic-stricken army dissolved in a disorderly retreat that even St. Clair confessed "was, in fact, a flight." More than 900 of the men involved were killed or wounded.[39]

When news of the catastrophe reached Washington, he was furious. St. Clair's defeat was a devastating blow to the administration and to Washington's prestige as a military leader. A congressional critic of the administration's western policy charged that the war had been "as unjustly undertaken as it has since been unwisely and unsuccessfully conducted." Congressmen who had no sympathy for the Indians were equally hostile to the idea of sending another army to face the Indians in the western wilderness. "It is only exposing our arms to disgrace," one congressman insisted, "betraying our own weakness, and lessening the public confidence in the General Government, to send forth armies to be butchered in the forests."[40]

The House of Representatives convened the first special investigative committee in its history to determine the causes of St. Clair's debacle. Angry congressmen demanded that the administration seek a negotiated settlement. Others insisted that the army assume a defensive posture. Even Senator Benjamin Hawkins of North Carolina, normally a supporter of the administration, privately urged Washington to make peace. "We seem to have forgotten altogether the right of the Indians," he complained. But Hawkins' challenge only hardened Washington's resolve to win. "We are involved in actual War!" he replied. Recalling his experience as a militia colonel defending the Virginia frontier in the

French and Indian War, Washington argued that a purely defensive posture "is not only impracticable against such an enemy, but the expence attending it would be ruinous." He saw no alternative to carrying the war once more into Indian country. The administration proposed to double the size of the army for the second time in a year and to outfit a new expedition to suppress the hostile tribes. After a fierce debate in Congress, Hawkins and a few others changed their votes, and the army bill passed by a narrow margin.[41]

Having obtained congressional approval for a new expedition, Washington had to choose a general to command it. No other appointment ever gave him as much anxiety. Washington preferred "Light-Horse Harry" Lee, the governor of Virginia, but Lee had been a colonel in the Revolutionary War, so finding experienced general officers willing to serve under him would pose an almost insurmountable problem. Washington's choice fell instead on Anthony Wayne, who had served as a brigadier general in the Continental Army.

Wayne was an extraordinary choice. He was headstrong and vain, and had a reputation for heavy drinking, all of which Washington deplored. But he was also extraordinarily brave and ambitious, and shared Washington's conviction that nothing short of military victory was likely to bring peace to the Northwest. Many congressmen were appalled by the nomination, but the Senate had never refused an army commission to one of Washington's nominees. Wayne was confirmed, though, as James Madison wrote, the appointment ran "rather against the bristles." It turned out to be one of the best appointments Washington ever made.[42]

A third defeat probably would have resulted in the loss of the West. St. Clair's humiliation had demonstrated the weakness of the American army to British and Spanish officials, and they responded by encouraging the Indians to increase their attacks on American settlements. The British renewed old proposals to establish an Indian buffer state in the Ohio Valley and refused to engage in further discussion about the future of the posts. It began to appear that the British intended to retain them indefinitely. The Spanish governor at New Orleans, Hector de Carondelet, concluded a new treaty with McGillivray promising arms and assistance if the Creeks would renew their war against the United States. "The conduct of Spain in this business," Washington wrote to Knox from Mount Vernon in the dismal summer of 1792, "is so unprovoked (by any event that has come to my knowledge), so misterious, and so hostile in appearance, that . . .

the mind can scarcely realize a procedure so base and inhuman." In September 1792 the southern tribes launched a major attack on the Cumberland River settlements. Nothing but the confusion among the southern chiefs after McGillivray's death the following February seems to have saved the United States from a general Indian war in the South.[43]

Washington was determined not to repeat earlier mistakes. Unlike Harmar and St. Clair, Wayne would not have to depend on undisciplined militia. He was given command of a regular army with an authorized strength of some 5,000 men, though his effective command generally numbered little more than half that number. Wayne established his base at Pittsburgh, and drilled his recruits endlessly, training his men to stand against the fierce attacks he knew they would face.

Wayne transferred his army to Fort Washington in 1793. By then the outbreak of a general European war had complicated the frontier situation. With Britain and France at war, Washington was reluctant to provoke the British by marching on the northwestern tribes. While Wayne drilled his army, the administration tried to negotiate peace with the Indians. Washington expected little to come of these efforts, having concluded that the Indians had become the instruments of a "concerted plan" of Britain and Spain "to check the growth of this rising Country."[44] Two emissaries sent to invite the hostile chiefs to a peace conference were killed. Others turned back without reaching their goal. A proposed peace conference in the summer of 1793 came to nothing. The three American commissioners Washington sent to meet with the Indians were stopped by the British at Niagara. They were hospitably treated, but kept away from the Indians while British advisers met with the hostile chiefs and persuaded them to insist on the withdrawal of all Americans from the right bank of the Ohio. The commissioners could not agree to such a retreat, and returned to Philadelphia without accomplishing anything.

Despite Washington's best efforts to preserve peace with the European powers, by early 1794 it seemed likely that the United States would shortly be at war with Britain, Spain, or both. In the Northwest it was becoming apparent that the British were working to ensure an Indian victory. In a speech to an Indian delegation in February 1794, the governor of Canada, Lord Dorchester, announced that he expected the United States and Britain to be at war within the year, and that Britain would fight to restore the Ohio River as the boundary between the Indians and the Americans. It was as close to a declaration of war as a colonial governor could come, and so outraged Congress that Washington was hard pressed to prevent measures that would lead irretrievably to war. Underscoring their determination to support the Indians, the British began building an advance fort on the Maumee River, blocking the route Wayne would have to follow through the agricultural heart of the Indian confederation.

Washington faced a crisis in the South as well, where it became increasingly difficult to restrain frontiersmen from attacking the Spaniards in an effort to take control of the Mississippi. Revolutionary War hero George Rogers Clark was preparing to lead Kentuckians down the Mississippi to seize New Orleans. Bracing for war, Governor Carondelet ordered the construction of an advance post on the American side of the Mississippi at Chickasaw Bluffs—later Memphis—and another on the Tombigbee River, deep inside United States territory. Washington issued a proclamation ordering the private armies to disperse, but it was clear that the patience of the westerners was exhausted. Growing defiance of federal law, particularly the hated whiskey excise, was symptomatic of collapsing federal authority in the West.

Nothing but a victory by Wayne seemed likely to restore federal authority in the western country. Under these circumstances Washington instructed Wayne not to let the British army stand between his troops and victory over the Indians. If the British intervened, he authorized Wayne to attack them: if forced to choose between a victory that would preserve the Union and peace with Britain, Washington did not hesitate to choose victory.

Despite two years of preparation, Wayne faced an extraordinary task. His advance post was at the end of long, vulnerable supply line. Western Pennsylvania, through which further supplies must come, was in open insurrection against the federal government. Kentucky was on the verge of inciting a war with Spain in his rear. The Indian force assembled to oppose him was the most formidable ever gathered, and included warriors from nearly every tribe between the Great Lakes and the Gulf of Mexico. They were led once more by Little Turtle, and furnished with transportation, arms, ammunition, and other supplies by the British Army.

After leaving men behind to guard his supply line, Wayne marched northward in July 1794 with no more than 1,500 regulars and an equal number of mounted militia. Facing them were more than 1,500 warriors. Wayne's army soon reached the fields and orchards along the Maumee River upon which Indians depended for subsistence. His men destroyed Indian villages and set fire to Indian cornfields as they marched, and established forts at strategic points along their route. Unlike Harmar and St. Clair, Wayne carefully guarded against ambush. The Indians, looking for an opportunity to surprise their opponents, could only watch in frustration. The two forces finally met in pitched battle a few miles from the British fort on the Maumee. On August 20, 1794, Wayne's disciplined army routed the hostile warriors in the Battle of Fallen Timbers. The retreating Indians sought refuge in the British fort, but the commander refused to open the gates. Left to defend themselves, the Indians fled in a disorganized mass down the river.

Wayne's victory broke the power of the hostile tribes and left them no choice but to make peace. The Treaty of Greenville, concluded in August 1795, secured the eastern portion of the Northwest Territory for the United States. As Washington had anticipated, the British surrendered the disputed posts once the United States demonstrated the ability and will to assert authority over its western territory. In 1795 the United States finally took possession of the posts, which many had believed would never be surrendered except in war. Washington's restrained but determined approach to the problem was vindicated. American success on the frontier also compelled Spain to settle its disputes with the United States. By the terms of Pinckney's Treaty, completed in October 1795, Spain abandoned its advance forts on the east bank of the Mississippi, and granted American citizens the free navigation of the river and the right to ship goods through the port of New Orleans. These treaties, and the American policies that lay behind them, laid the foundation for the United States as a continental republic.

At the outset of the Washington presidency, few Americans dared to imagine that the United States as a continental republic extending to the Mississippi River and beyond. Some reasoned that the conflicting economic interests of East and West would lead to sectional discord that would weaken the bonds of the Union. Many thought that the Indian war on the northwest frontier was a senseless waste of resources—that the United States could not possibly people the vast interior space between the Appalachians and the Mississippi in less than a century, and that in the process, the eastern seaboard states would be depopulated, leading to labor shortages and high wages. Most advocates of American manufacturing were unenthusiastic about westward expansion because they feared it would depopulate the East and lead to high labor costs that would make it impossible for American goods to compete with European imports. Some landowners in the East feared that the opening of vast new acres in the West would undermine the market value of their property. Many eastern merchants were skeptical of the value of westward expansion because it would draw people and capital away from the seaboard port cities. Others worried that the culture of a continental republic, dominated by the frontier and agrarian population of the interior, would be coarse and unrefined.

Washington shared none of this gloomy pessimism about the political, economic, and cultural consequences of western expansion. He was confident that Americans would inevitably people the West and as President he sought to facilitate this westward movement of the American population. Few things Washington achieved as President had a greater immediate impact on American life than the hard-won victory on the northwest frontier. When Washington assumed the presidency, there were barely any permanent settlers in the Ohio Valley. Within a decade of the battle of Fallen Timbers, Ohio had become a state and had a population greater than that of most of the colonies at the time of the Revolution. By 1820 it was home to over half a million people, making it the fifth-largest state. Many thousands more poured into the Indiana and Illinois territories, and into the southern interior, into what would become the states of Tennessee, Alabama, and Mississippi. In the twenty years after Washington left office, the American people occupied more new territory than they had occupied in the entire seventeenth and eighteenth centuries.[45]

George Washington was not responsible for this extraordinary movement of the American people. But he anticipated it more clearly than any of his peers, never wavered in his determination to clear the way for western settlement, and helped ensure that the new states formed in the West would be firmly attached to the American Union and not held in sway by Britain or Spain. He was confident that American settlers on what his generation called the "western waters" could be bound to Americans on the eastern side of the Appalachians by indissoluble ties of economic interest, and that these ties would strengthen the Union and secure the future of the United States as a continental nation.

CHAPTER FOUR
WASHINGTON'S CITY

GEORGE WASHINGTON'S VISION OF THE UNITED States as a vast
commercial empire shaped one of the most ambitious projects of his
presidency—the establishment of a new city on the Potomac River,
designed and constructed as the permanent capital of the republic. The
founding of Washington, D.C., is among the most enduring
accomplishments of the Washington presidency. It was also one of the
most controversial. George Washington was determined to make the
city a symbol of the Union and a source of pride for the nation, but the
project was marred from the start by disputes, disappointments, and
financial distress. When the federal government occupied the city in
1800, its officials were greeted by a tangle of unpaved streets littered
with the stumps of recently felled trees. There was almost no housing
available for congressmen. Indeed, there were only a few buildings of
any sort in the mile separating the unfinished Capitol and President's
House. Most unbiased observers regarded the city as a colossal failure, a
judgment echoed by visitors for most of the following century.

The founding of the city was the culmination of George
Washington's lifelong involvement with the development of the
Potomac Valley, the economic diversification of the Upper South, and
the opening of the trans-Appalachian West. He had long been
convinced that the Potomac Valley was destined by nature to become
the center of American commerce. Almost alone among the rivers that
flow into the Atlantic, the Potomac penetrates far into the Appalachian
barrier and offered a potential commercial route from the Ohio Valley
to the eastern seaboard. In Washington's generation the river was
navigable by seagoing ships as far as Georgetown, Maryland, but above

---

Mount Vernon on the shore of the Potomac River. *Washington's conviction that the Potomac
River would become the commercial avenue to the Ohio Valley shaped his decision to place
the nation's capital a few miles north of Mount Vernon.*

that port it was blocked by falls and ran through shallows strewn with boulders. Washington believed that by building canals around the falls and removing obstructions the river could be made navigable by shallow-draft boats far to the west, where it could be linked by short roads to streams flowing into the Ohio River.

The idea that the Potomac River would one day become the principal artery of trade between the Ohio Valley and the East had occupied Washington's thinking since he was a young man. His elder half-brother Lawrence, from whom he inherited Mount Vernon, had been one of the organizers of the Ohio Company, formed in 1747 to exploit the Potomac route to the Ohio. Lawrence and other Ohio Company promoters were involved in the establishment of Alexandria, chartered in 1749, which they envisioned as a clearinghouse for the goods of the trans-Appalachian West. As a seventeen year-old surveyor, George Washington prepared a plat of the new town. During the French and Indian War, he proposed clearing some of the rocks from the main channel to make it possible to bring supply vessels up the river. Sensing the potential for profit, after that war he claimed thousands of acres of bounty lands along the Ohio River. As a member of the House of Burgesses in the 1760s, he championed a proposal to clear the Potomac.

The Revolutionary War interrupted these efforts, but after the war Washington assumed the presidency of the Potomac Company, chartered by Virginia and Maryland to open the navigation of the river. The company began building canals around the falls and clearing channels through the rocky shallows to make the river navigable by flat-bottomed barges. Although the Potomac Company was not directly involved in industrial development, the canal around the Great Falls was expected to facilitate efforts to harness the water power of the falls to drive the wheels of industrial production. The endowments of nature, Washington believed, made the Potomac the ideal location for a great city that would become the political, commercial, and industrial center of the new nation.

The idea of building a new city to be the permanent seat of the federal government was not original to Washington, but its location and character were shaped mainly by his vision of a great city rising on the Potomac. During the Revolutionary War and the Confederation period that followed, the United States did not have a fixed seat of government. Congress met first in Philadelphia, but during and after the war it convened in several other places between Annapolis and New

York City. Members grew tired of moving from place to place, meeting in borrowed rooms, and enduring the whims of state and local officials. In 1783 they voted to establish a permanent federal seat.

But the Confederation Congress possessed neither the money nor the political will to carry out the plan, which immediately became mired in an intractable debate over the proper location. Everyone agreed that the federal seat should be located somewhere in the center of the nation, but Congress seemed unable to decide whether this should be the geographical center, the center of population, or even the center of wealth. Every place from New York City to the Potomac River seemed to have proponents. Congress reconsidered the matter occasionally during the course of the 1780s, as it migrated from Princeton to Annapolis to Trenton and finally, to New York City, but never reached any decision. As the impotent Confederation government faded into insignificance, the debate assumed a kind of comic irrelevance. A newspaper satirist suggested that Congress might as well establish its seat in the basket of a hot-air balloon, permanently drifting up and down the Atlantic seaboard.

The First Federal Congress took up the question of location shortly after Washington assumed the presidency, and quickly became just as deadlocked as the Confederation Congress had been. Southerners naturally preferred a location on the Potomac, but could not break the impasse without a few votes from the North. Congressmen from the interior of Pennsylvania preferred a site on or near the Susquehanna River. Robert Morris proposed Germantown, a suburb of Philadelphia. Trenton was suggested, and Baltimore was embraced temporarily and then cast aside as congressmen jockeyed for position. The dispute bared growing sectional tensions between North and South that Washington feared might destroy the Union.

The issue was settled by a political bargain. To mollify representatives from the northeastern states, proponents of a Potomac site agreed to Alexander Hamilton's proposal to have the federal government assume the outstanding Revolutionary War debts of the states. Residents of most of the southern states had nothing to gain from assumption, having paid off a large part of their debts with depreciated paper money. But Virginians, in particular, expected to reap considerable advantages from having the federal seat on the Potomac. The compromise—the first in a long series of political compromises between North and South—was arranged by Washington's congressional adviser and confidant, James Madison, with the cooperation of Thomas Jefferson and Alexander Hamilton.

Washington's role in these negotiations is not revealed in the documentary record. He was determined not to give the appearance of interfering in the legislative process. But members of Congress were well aware of his preference for building the new capital on the Potomac, and his views undoubtedly influenced the outcome of the debate. At least one congressman, Senator William Maclay of Pennsylvania, believed that Washington secretly orchestrated the compromise to gain the federal residence for the Potomac, but no evidence has been found to substantiate the charge. Regardless of his role in striking the bargain, Washington was pleased with the bill, though signing it exposed him to criticism that he had allowed his personal interest in the Potomac to influence his public conduct.[46]

During the years of debate over the location of the federal seat, there was never a sustained discussion of what the capital city should be like, or even whether the federal seat should be a city at all. The most doctrinaire republicans seem to have imagined a kind of government village—an American Acropolis isolated from the interest-ridden politics and corrupting influences of the major commercial cities, to which citizen-legislators would repair periodically to conduct the people's business. Moneyed men preferred to locate the government permanently in New York or Philadelphia, or somewhere close by, where they could keep an eye on it and ensure that it served the interests of American commerce.

The Residence Act, passed in July 1790, effectively turned the resolution of this question over to Washington. He envisioned a great city that would become the metropolis of the United States—a center of government, commerce and industry, education and culture—a city that would one day combine the ancient greatness of Athens and Rome with the modern greatness of London and Paris. The Residence Act granted the President sweeping authority with which to make this vision a reality. Under the terms of the law the federal government was to reside for ten years in Philadelphia, after which it would move to a new permanent seat to be constructed on the Potomac, inside a district ten miles square (encompassing 100 square miles) over which Congress would enjoy exclusive jurisdiction. The law left Washington to choose the specific location for the federal district and to appoint three commissioners, answerable to the President alone, to oversee the design and construction of the city.

Congress seems to have intended that the President would delegate direction of the project to the three commissioners, but Washington asserted personal control from the beginning and never relinquished it. He delayed appointing the commissioners until after he had made many of the important decisions himself. The commissioners he finally appointed—David Stuart, Thomas Johnson, and Daniel Carroll of Rock Creek—were men upon whose deference he could depend. Stuart was a personal friend and a member of Washington's extended family; he was married to the widow of Martha Washington's son, John Parke Custis. Johnson was a former governor of Maryland and a long-time associate of Washington's in the Potomac Company. Daniel Carroll of Rock Creek was a former congressman whose nephew and brother-in-law owned large tracts of land in the district.[47]

The area Washington chose for the federal district surrounded the junction of the Potomac River and the Eastern Branch (now called the Anacostia River), and included the ports of Georgetown and Alexandria. In the middle of this federal district, between Rock Creek and the Eastern Branch, was the area Washington envisioned for the city itself. The city site rose gradually from the river to an elevation of 100 feet, and was surrounded by a ring of hills that reached up to 400 feet, forming a kind of vast, natural amphitheater. The site was dotted with tobacco and grain fields, pastures, and woodlands, and crossed by a few roads linking scattered plantation houses. Low hills—the most prominent was Jenkins Hill where the Capitol would be built—offered sweeping views of the Potomac.

The city was not located on a swamp. As on any tidal river in the region, there were marshes where tidal creeks entered the Potomac, principally at the mouth of Tiber Creek, which flowed into the river a few hundred yards south of the site chosen for the President's House. But most of the federal district was dry and healthy. The charge that Washington was built on a swamp seems to have originated in the complaints of nineteenth-century northern congressman about the city's steamy summers, its muddy, unfinished streets, and the presence of slavery. The charge survived the end of slavery as a metaphor for political corruption.

The southern boundary of the district was less than nine miles north of Mount Vernon. By choosing a site so close to the estate and to other property he owned, Washington exposed himself to the charge that he was motivated by private interests. But he was prepared to face this criticism in order to secure a site that satisfied his ambition for a monumental city that could also become a great commercial and industrial center. The Eastern Branch appeared to provide an ideal anchorage, and the adjacent land, between the Eastern Branch and what would soon be called Capitol Hill, offered what seemed to be an ideal setting for commercial activity—low and level enough to facilitate the easy movement of goods, but high enough above the river to protect warehouses and other buildings from floods, and people from the diseases associated with many port cities. To the northwest of the city, the Great Falls of the Potomac seemed to offer an inexhaustible supply of power for industrial development. Such advantages, historian Kenneth Bowling concludes, led Washington to consider the junction of the Potomac and the Eastern Branch "the best spot for the survival of the Union to which so much of his life had been devoted." The commissioners named the city in Washington's honor in September 1791.[48]

To design his city, Washington chose French-born engineer Pierre L'Enfant. The engineer first designated the sites for the Capitol and the President's House and received Washington's approval. He based the rest of his plan, which he submitted to the President in August 1791, on these cardinal points. L'Enfant's conception of the city was grand. His plan called for a national capital covering almost ten square miles, much larger than any contemporary American city. Its principal buildings and public spaces were to be connected by a series of radiating "Grand transverse Avenues," 160 feet wide and flanked by tree-lined walks. These diagonal avenues, which L'Enfant superimposed over a conventional street grid, were to offer long vistas from one focal point to another. Merely paving the streets L'Enfant proposed would have consumed the entire budget of the federal government for several years. The proportions of the city bore no relationship to the foreseeable needs of the new republic.[49]

L'Enfant drew his inspiration—particularly for the grand diagonal avenues and the monumental vistas—from Versailles. But Americans did not need to look to Europe for models of city and town planning. The largest and most widely admired city in the United States, Philadelphia, was the product of a well-conceived urban plan. Its regular grid of streets and evenly distributed squares were applauded for their rationality and efficiency. But Philadelphia was more compact than the city L'Enfant proposed, and its construction had been spread out over a century. The Federal City had to be ready to receive the government in less than a decade.

Therein lay the problem. Although Congress had voted to move the

Pierre L'Enfant's ambitious plan for the nation's capital reflected Washington's lifelong determination to see a great city rise on the Potomac River.

capital to the Potomac after ten years, the actual commitment to do so was very weak. The Residence Act delegated responsibility for defining the district, laying out the city, and constructing the necessary government buildings to Washington and the three commissioners appointed by him, but Congress had not appropriated any money to carry out this work. Nor did Washington have any reason to believe that Congress would appropriate any money for the project. The Maryland and Virginia legislatures, as an incentive to locate the Federal City within their borders, had voted to provide $192,000 for the construction of federal buildings. This promise was initially all that Washington had with which to make the Federal City a reality.

To overcome the initial financial challenge, Washington suggested a novel scheme to the planters and merchants who owned land where the Federal City was to be built. Meeting with these "original proprietors" in Georgetown in the spring of 1791, Washington proposed that they deed their land to neutral trustees. The city would then be laid out and each landowner would be given half of his original acreage back in city lots, which would have more potential value than their original holdings. The federal government would retain the rest of the lots, and sell most of them to raise money to construct the federal buildings and to make other necessary public improvements. Anxious to secure the advantages

55

of having the Federal City located on their land, the proprietors agreed. Many of them expected that the sale of their lots would make them wealthy.[50]

L'Enfant told the President that he did not believe the sale of lots would provide the funds needed to construct the city, and argued that piecemeal sales of land would fragment development and make it difficult to control. He urged the President to borrow the needed money, which would make speedy development of the city possible. Events later proved L'Enfant right, but Washington regarded borrowing as politically impossible, and was not prepared to debate the matter. L'Enfant would have to work with such funds as the commissioners were able to secure. When L'Enfant refused to accept the authority of the commissioners, Washington dismissed him.[51]

Thereafter Washington expressed his determination to leave the management of the project to the commissioners. But this determination quickly faded. Washington involved himself almost constantly in the affairs of the city. Almost no detail escaped his attention. A year after L'Enfant's dismissal, the commissioners fired his successor. Washington requested his reinstatement. Washington oversaw everything from the design details of the Capitol to the type of stone upon which iron fences should be mounted. He advised the commissioners on even minor modifications to the city plan.

No amount of attention could save the project from financial troubles. The money from Maryland and Virginia was only a fraction of what was needed for the federal buildings. The sale of city lots never produced the expected revenue, though Washington attended some of the sales and bid on lots himself when interest began to wane. In frustration the President and the commissioners embraced proposals from real estate speculators to purchase large blocks of property. James Greenleaf of Massachusetts contracted to buy 3,000 lots at $66.50 each and promised to lend the commissioners $2,200 a month until 1800. A year later Greenleaf and his partners, Robert Morris and John Nicholson, sold 500 of the lots to Thomas Law for four times what they paid. But the city offered investors few opportunities this good. Greenleaf prudently withdrew from the partnership in 1795, but Morris and Nicholson forged blindly ahead. Unable to sell their lots and pressed by the federal government and private creditors, they wound up in debtor's prison. In 1795 Washington finally turned to the Maryland legislature, which agreed to lend the commissioners the money needed to complete the federal buildings.

There were construction problems as well. The first major structure, a stone bridge spanning lower Rock Creek, was so poorly designed that it collapsed. Washington praised the design submitted for the Capitol by Dr. William Thornton, a self-taught architect, for the "Grandeur, Simplicity, and Beauty of the exterior; the propriety with which the apartments are distributed; and the economy in the whole mass of the structure." Thomas Jefferson, a skilled architect himself, was nearly as effusive. But after consultation with professional architects Jefferson concluded that the design was defective: some of the columns were too widely spaced to support the mass above, a colonnade in the middle of the grand conference room obstructed the view, but if it were removed the ceiling would collapse, and an important floor lacked any means of support. There were other problems with the design, but with time passing quickly Washington directed Jefferson to have the problems worked out, and laid the cornerstone in an elaborate Masonic ceremony in September 1793.[52]

Through all of these troubles, Washington maintained a seemingly unrealistic optimism about the future of the city. It was as if he believed he could make it rise by force of will. In September 1793 he wrote to Tobias Lear that the city "could not well fail under any circumstances." A few weeks later he wrote to English agriculturalist Arthur Young that "The federal City . . . is encreasing fast in buildings, and rising into consequence; and will, I have no doubt, from the advantages given to it by nature, and its proximity to a rich interior country, and the western territory, become the emporium of the United States." Confident in the city's future, Washington invested in several lots in different parts of the capital for himself, and bought adjoining ones on a hillside where he planned to construct a fine house and garden.[53]

Washington's confidence in the future of the city was not widely shared. The skeptical wife of a contractor complained that the city was infested with "dolts, delvers, magicians, soothsayers, quacks, bankrupts, puffs, speculators, monopolizers, extortioners, traitors, petit foggy lawyers, and ham bricklayers." Many Americans simply refused to believe that the government would ever move to the unfinished city. Pennsylvanians, determined to keep the federal government in Philadelphia indefinitely, constructed a spacious house for the President. Washington refused to occupy it.[54]

Nearly every contemporary commentator believed that the project was too ambitious to succeed. The Duke de La Rochefoucauld-Liancourt visited the site in 1797 and dismissed the whole thing. "The plan," he wrote, "is fine, cleverly and grandly designed, but it is its very grandeur, its magnificence, which causes it to be nothing but a dream." Even the men involved in carrying out the plan ultimately despaired. Benjamin Henry Latrobe, involved in building the Capitol, described "the idea of creating a new city, better arranged in its local distribution of houses and streets, more magnificent in its public buildings, and superior in the advantages of its site" as "the favorite folly of General Washington." It had become, he concluded in 1806, a "Gigantic Abortion."[55]

In the fall of 1799 the commissioners informed Washington's successor, John Adams, that the Federal City was ready to receive the government. George Washington seems never to have doubted that this day would come. On December 8, 1799—less than a week before his death—Washington wrote to William Thornton that "by the obstructions continually thrown in its way, by friends or enemies, this City has had to pass through a firey trial. Yet, I trust will, ultimately, escape the Ordeal with Éclat."[56]

A year later the government took up residence in the city. Treasury Secretary Oliver Wolcott was shocked at the rude, unfinished state of the place, the "immense sums . . . squandered in buildings which are but partly finished, in situations which are not, and never will be the scenes of business, while the parts, near the public buildings, are almost wholly unimproved." It was a dismal place, reported John Randolph, "where the wretched exile is cut off from all information, society or amusement, and where the common necessaries of life can be procured not without difficulty, and the most enormous expence." Albert Gallatin said that the unfinished city was uniformly hated by members of both parties, and his wife predicted that the city "never will be of any consequence, even if the national government should remain there." For the next seventy years Congress periodically debated moving the nation's capital somewhere else—back to Philadelphia, to Cincinnati, to St. Louis—but the debates, and the federal government, never went anywhere.[57]

George Washington's belief that the Potomac Valley was destined to become the center of American commerce proved mistaken, though his reasoning was sound. The port that captured the largest share of the trade of the Ohio country did indeed become the commercial capital of the republic. But that port, as events unfolded, was New York. The Hudson River and the Erie Canal proved a more efficient route to transport goods of the Old Northwest to the Atlantic market, and this trade route established New York as the nerve center of American capitalism.

The city of Washington remained an economic backwater throughout the nineteenth century. The idea of improving the navigation of the Potomac River to carry the commerce of the Ohio Valley down to the Chesapeake Bay was abandoned as unfeasible shortly after Washington's death. A subsequent effort to build a canal from the national capital to the Ohio stalled when construction reached Cumberland, Maryland. The water power of the Great Falls of the Potomac was never harnessed to drive the mills of the Industrial Revolution. An 1830 visitor commented that the city was marked by a "total absence of all sights, sounds, or smells of commerce." Fifty years after George Washington's death a French visitor found a city composed of "streets without houses, and of houses without streets." Its fate, he wrote, was "a striking proof of this truth that one cannot create a great city at will."[58]

But Washington had not expected the city to realize its potential within fifty years. As in so many other cases, he planned for a distant posterity, when the power and importance of the United States would justify a capital city of such grand proportions. "A Century hence," he wrote to Sally Fairfax on May 16, 1798, "if this Country keeps united (and it is surely its policy and Interest to do so) will produce a City— though not as large as London—yet of a magnitude inferior to few others in Europe, on the Banks of the Potomack." More than two centuries later, the city has not realized all of Washington's ambitions. But it has long since become a symbol of the Union and a source of pride for the nation, and has assumed its place among the great cities of the world, as Washington expected that it would.[59]

CHAPTER FIVE
THE CHALLENGE OF PARTISANSHIP

GEORGE WASHINGTON PRESIDED OVER THE FEDERAL government during a period of intense political passion, shaped by revolutionary idealism and anxieties engendered by the uncertainties of building a continental nation on the untried basis of popular consent. The American Revolution had established the independence of the United States and replaced a monarchical form of government with a republic, but the future character and form of that republic remained unclear. Americans of the post-Revolutionary period were obsessively concerned about the fragility of republican government. Their political discourse was dominated by hysterical exaggeration, irrational fears of conspiracy, and apocalyptic anxieties that led them to believe that the fate of republican liberty depended on what now seem to have been the most mundane decisions. Washington's greatest challenge as president was to prevent this political passion, and the political partisanship it engendered, from undermining or even destroying the Union.[60]

Keeping political divisions from tearing the Union apart required a good bit of political dexterity, especially since the challenge did not take the form or come from the quarter that Washington had expected. At the outset of his administration he was concerned that opponents to the ratification of the Federal Constitution would form parties within the states, agitating against the exercise of federal authority and the establishment of an energetic national government. He expected this opposition to be organized on the state level and to work for the restoration of state power. He could hardly have imagined that the opposition would be formed within the federal government, and that its principal leader would be a member of his own administration.

Washington's principal subordinates, Thomas Jefferson and Alexander Hamilton, did not know one another before they met in New

Fishing Tin. Washington's pocket fishing kit is a reminder of his three-day fishing trip with Thomas Jefferson and Alexander Hamilton in the summer of 1790. Sharpened barbs of another sort soon made enemies of Washington's two most improtant subordinates.

York in the spring of 1790 and they approached each other with a caution that moved quickly on through suspicion to mutual hatred. Their antagonism was fueled by personal differences—clashing ambitions, social animosities, and mutual misunderstandings—but at bottom it was based on profoundly different ideas about the future of the new republic, the character it should assume, and the sort of men who should lead it. The conflict between them led, over the course of the Washington administration, to the formation of contending political parties—Hamiltonian Federalists and Jeffersonian Republicans—within the federal government.

Hamilton was a revolutionary whose ultimate aim was to transform the established social order by making it genuinely open to merit. American society, as Hamilton saw it, was dominated by an entrenched elite whose status depended upon family connections, inherited wealth, and land ownership. Hamilton himself had risen to prominence through the patronage of this elite, but he had concluded that the rigid social order it dominated offered insufficient opportunities for achievement or rewards for industry. In fact it encouraged indolence. Hamilton's purpose was to transform this society by using the authority of a strong centralized state to accelerate commercialization. In a commercial society, Hamilton perceived, status was derived from the marketplace, where ideas and goods were valued impartially. A commercial order, he believed, was the one most suited to a modern republic. Hamilton regarded the financial system of Great Britain, the most commercially advanced nation in Europe, as the most useful model for the United States.[61]

Jefferson, by contrast, regarded the increasing commercial orientation of American life as a symptom of moral decay that would make it impossible to maintain a republican form of government. Commercial society, Jefferson believed, robbed men of their personal independence by making them dependent on others and tying them to debt. He regarded powerful centralized governments as inevitably corrupt—that their use of patronage and financial influence constituted a legalized form of bribery. Jefferson idealized the independent yeoman farmer, whom he imagined as self-sufficient and consequently incorruptible, and favored policies that would maintain the existing agrarian nature of American society indefinitely. His experience as a diplomat in Europe confirmed his biases against urban commercial society and strong centralized state power. The mass poverty of Europe and the corresponding callousness and corruption of Europe's nobility appalled him. He regarded Great Britain, with its centralized financial system, national debt, and standing army with abhorrence, and saw Hamilton's efforts to replicate its centralized system of finance as the first steps toward imposing a monarchy on the people of the United States.

This clash of ideas was exacerbated by differences in ability, style, and habits of mind. Jefferson possessed stunning intellectual breadth, but his political ideas were surprisingly rigid and his mind was haunted by conspiratorial fantasies. He was a generous friend, but in public he was awkward and humorless. In a situation that called for a good deal of political subtlety, Jefferson was constitutionally incapable of keeping things to himself, never understood whom he should trust, and constantly gave his confidence to men who sided with Hamilton. He expressed himself brilliantly in writing, but was frustrated by the rapid give and take of political deal-making. "I do not understand bargaining nor possess the dexterity requisite to make them," he confessed to Madison. And he loathed confrontation.[62]

Most of these characteristics put Jefferson at a disadvantage in his dispute with Hamilton. The Secretary of the Treasury was brilliant and charming, and won political adherents readily. His knowledge of public finance was profound, and he accomplished his work at a pace that confused his opponents and forced them to move quickly to meet him on his own ground.

But his program had serious political liabilities. In the short run, it required the support of traditional aristocratic proprietary wealth, which opened Hamilton up to the charge of favoring the interests of the prevailing oligarchies. It also required the cultivation of a close commercial relationship with Britain, which exposed him and his supporters to the dominant post-revolutionary spirit of anglophobia. That anglophobia was especially strong in the South, particularly in Washington's own Virginia.

To make matters worse, Hamilton had an obsessive concern for his reputation as a man of honor and integrity, and could not resist the desire to defend himself from the slightest attacks on his character and conduct. He did so with complete effectiveness. But the devastating way Hamilton dispatched his critics left people with the gnawing suspicion that a man so extraordinarily capable of defending himself must have something to hide.

Washington never doubted Hamilton's public-spiritedness or integrity. He personally favored a commercial order over Jefferson's agrarianism, and had no patience with Jefferson's view that the Hamilton financial system was the entering wedge of a conspiracy to impose a monarchy on the United States. The economic and philosophical basis for the conflict between the two men was probably beyond Washington's grasp, but he understood its political implications better than either of them. In its political dynamics, the conflict was essentially sectional. Washington recognized that, whatever its long-term consequences, Hamilton's program appeared to serve the immediate interests of the more commercially advanced North at the expense of the almost entirely agrarian South and West. Washington wisely perceived that his job was not to choose between them—something both men tried to force him to do—but to attempt to conciliate them for as long as possible and prevent the controversy from engendering popular unrest or sectional conflict. Regardless of his personal sentiments, he studiously avoided becoming a Hamiltonian partisan, and sought to build consensus among his subordinates.

Washington despised political partisanship. "If we mean to support the Liberty and Independence which it has cost us so much blood and treasure to establish," he wrote in 1790, "we must drive far away the demon of party spirit." He did not foresee the development of national parties that would reach into every corner of every state in a competition for control of the central government. Washington subscribed to the common pre-modern view that political parties and factions were subversive and disruptive, and those who fomented them were wicked men intent on pursuing their private interests at the expense of the peace and good order of society. The idea of a legitimate opposition party—a standing party specifically organized to oppose the policies of the existing government and even to displace that government by peaceful means—did not take shape until after Washington's death. It would have appalled him.[63]

Washington envisioned a unified political community in which local interests and partisan sentiments would be set aside in the national interest. In his First Inaugural Address, he pledged that "no local prejudices, or attachments; no separate views, nor party animosities, will misdirect the comprehensive and equal eye which ought to watch over this great Assemblage of communities and interests." He saw his own task as fulfilling the role of what the English political theorist Henry St. John, Viscount Bolingbroke, called the "Patriot King"—a benevolent leader above faction or party, who could, "without violence to his people, renew the spirit of liberty in their minds" by banishing corruption and by "rendering public virtue and real capacity the sole means of acquiring any degree of power or profit in the state." The ideal "Patriot King," according to Bolingbroke, would "govern like the common father of his people" who would be "united by one common interest and animated by one common spirit."[64]

For the first two years of Washington's first term, a common spirit seemed to prevail within the administration. Jefferson assumed office in March 1790, and for most of the next year he and Hamilton cooperated as fully as Washington could have wished. Jefferson was a spectator to the adoption of most of Hamilton's financial system, but did not voice any serious dissent. The rapid succession of programs coming from the treasury seems to have bewildered him. Not until the beginning of 1791 did Jefferson reach the dark conclusion that the treasury secretary was replicating the major features of British fiscal policy in order to subvert the Federal Constitution and replace it with a government based on the British model. From that moment Jefferson dedicated himself to purging Hamilton from the administration.

Washington did not begin to realize the extent of Jefferson's hostility to Hamilton's policies until early in 1792, when Jefferson privately warned him that "the department of treasury possessed already such an influence as to swallow up the whole Executive powers." Hamilton's financial system, Jefferson asserted, was seducing the people into "a species of gambling, destructive of morality, & which had introduced its poison into the government itself." Members of Congress had "feathered their nests" by speculating in government securities. These same members—loyal minions of Hamilton—had voted for every measure that would serve their private interests. Hamilton's new proposal for government subsidies to encourage manufacturing, Jefferson insisted, proved that he was attempting to subvert the Constitution and create a centralized government of unlimited power.[65]

Jefferson's charges were soon repeated and amplified in a series of anonymous articles, signed "Brutus," in Philip Freneau's new *National Gazette*. Although Washington was not aware of it, Jefferson and Madison had recruited Freneau—a veteran editor with a bottomless talent for slander and coarse invective—to start the *National Gazette* as an alternative to John Fenno's *Gazette of the United States*, which was a steady supporter of Hamilton and his program. As inducements, Jefferson had given Freneau a post as translating clerk in the state department and promised him privileged information on foreign affairs. The letters of "Brutus" were the opening blast in a newspaper war with

Hamilton and his partisans.

Washington was deeply disturbed by the unexpected outburst of partisan rancor. He had long looked forward to retiring at the end of his first term, and his determination to do so became more fixed in the early months of 1792. In May he asked James Madison to help him frame a valedictory address to the American people—the germ of the Farewell Address Washington would leave the nation in 1796. He explained to Madison that he would remain in office only if his departure would leave the country embroiled in a serious political crisis resulting from the "divided opinions which seem to prevail at present." Madison urged Washington to reconsider, and all of Washington's department heads urged him to accept another term. Hamilton and Jefferson each viewed Washington as their only protection from the partisan intrigues of the other. Hamilton insisted that Washington was the only person who could save the Union from its enemies.[66]

Jefferson combined his appeal with the severest attack on Hamilton he had yet laid before the President. Jefferson assured Washington that he sympathized with his desire to quit the public stage, but that the efforts of Hamilton and his "corrupt squadron" in Congress to subvert the republic and erect a monarchy in its place had clouded the public mind with doubts and fears about the future of the republic. Under the circumstances Washington's continued leadership was needed to preserve the Union. "I can scarcely contemplate a more incalculable evil," Jefferson wrote, "than the breaking of the union into two or more parts." Yet considering the strength of Antifederalism in the South, and the fact that Hamilton's financial system favored the creditor classes of the North at the expense of southern planters and small farmers, Jefferson predicted the secession of the South if Washington retired. But, he added, "North and South will hang together, if they have you to hang on."[67]

Disunion was one of Washington's greatest fears, but he believed that it was more likely to result from the agitation of the opposition than from Hamilton's financial system. He met with Jefferson on July 10, 1792, and told him that the "suspicions against a particular party . . . had been carried a great deal too far." He was unmoved by Jefferson's warning that Hamilton's program would lead to the dissolution of the Union. He had toured the country himself, he pointed out, and had "found the people happy and contented." With typical indirection, Washington made the opposition press, rather than Jefferson and his colleagues, the object of his displeasure. He warned Jefferson that articles published in the *National Gazette* seemed intended to stir up opposition to the government, and cited recent excise disturbances in western Pennsylvania as a consequence of this sort of agitation. Such disturbances threatened "a separation of the Union," and this, rather than Hamilton's financial program, would lead to anarchy and finally, the very thing Jefferson feared, "a resort to monarchical government."

Washington also made it clear that he regarded the attack on Hamilton's program as an attack on himself. "He considered those papers as attacking him directly," Jefferson wrote, "for he must be a fool indeed to swallow the little sugar plumbs here & there thrown out to him. That in condemning the administration of the government they condemned him, for if they thought there were measures pursued contrary to his sentiment, they must conceive him too careless to attend to them or too stupid to understand them. That tho he indeed he had signed many acts which he did not approve in all their parts, yet he had never put his name to one which he did not think on the whole was eligible."[68]

Washington laid Jefferson's accusations before Hamilton in a letter written at Mount Vernon on July 29, 1792. According to Hamilton's critics, Washington explained, the "ultimate object" of Hamilton's financial program "is to prepare the way for a change, from the present republican form of Government, to that of a monarchy; of which the British Constitution is to be the model." Washington pretended as if these charges had been made by men, like George Mason, who were not "friendly . . . to the government" and were "disposed to arraign the conduct of its Officers." This bit of misdirection could not have fooled anyone, and Washington could not have expected that it would. Washington made no real attempt to disguise the identity of Hamilton's accuser; he quoted Jefferson's letter at length and paraphrased the rest. As Washington undoubtedly intended, Hamilton instantly recognized his unnamed antagonist. The next day Hamilton launched a series of attacks on Jefferson in the *Gazette of the United States*.[69]

Though providing confidential information to Hamilton fueled the conflict, Washington still hoped to reconcile his subordinates. He wrote to Jefferson from Mount Vernon on August 23, 1792, in an effort to end the "internal dissensions . . . harrowing and tearing our vitals." Without "more charity for opinions and acts of one another in Governmental matters," Washington insisted, "it will be difficult, if not impracticable, to manage the Reins of Government." The result could only be that the government would be "torn asunder." Washington wrote similarly to Hamilton and to Attorney General Edmund Randolph a few days later. To both of them, Washington was explicit about the consequences of the conflict for the Union. Without mutual forbearance, he wrote, he did not see "how the Union of the States can be much longer preserved."[70]

Hamilton confessed to Washington that he was responsible for some of the newspaper attacks on Jefferson, but explained that he believed himself "the deeply injured party." He outlined the wrongs Jefferson had committed: "I *know* that I have been an object of uniform opposition from Mr. Jefferson from the first moment of his coming to the City of New York to enter upon his present office. . . . I have long seen a formed party in the Legislature, under his auspices, bent upon my subversion. I cannot doubt, from the evidence I possess, that the *National Gazette* was instituted by him for political purpose," chief among which was "to render me and all the measures connected with my department as odious as possible." Hamilton nonetheless promised to follow any plan for reconciliation that Washington might propose, and suggested that if it should fail, the public good might be best served by replacing both men.[71]

Jefferson gave no ground at all. Hamilton, he insisted, was at the head of a faction formed "for the purpose of subverting step by step the principles of the constitution." Hamilton had interfered in the business of the state department and had made false charges against him in the newspapers. Jefferson's disdain for Hamilton also included a particularly unattractive element of social snobbery. Alluding to Hamilton's illegitimate birth in the West Indies and financial dependence on his government appointment, Jefferson concluded that he would not allow his own reputation "to be clouded by the slanders of a man whose history, from the moment at which history can stoop to notice him, is a tissue of machinations against the liberty of the country which has not only received and given him bread, but heaped it's honors on his head." Jefferson stopped at Mount Vernon on his way to Philadelphia in October 1792 and repeated his charges. Washington responded that there were not "ten men in the U.S. whose opinions were worth attention" who held "the idea of transforming this government into a monarchy." Jefferson assured Washington that he was wrong.[72]

From that moment Washington must have known that an accommodation between the two sides was impossible. This realization, as much as anything else, probably convinced Washington of the necessity of serving a second term, for only he could have prevented the rupture within the government from leading to dissolution of the Union. Attorney General Edmund Randolph predicted that factional violence and even civil war would result if he refused re-election. He urged the President that it would be "much easier . . . to disperse the factions, which are rushing to this catastrophe, than to subdue them, after they shall appear in arms."[73]

By the summer of 1792, opponents of Hamilton's programs were calling themselves Republicans. The opposition drew adherents from all parts of the country, but it was particularly strong among southerners. The planter aristocracy and the small farmers of the region were more often antagonists than allies, but the Hamiltonian program united them against what a Virginian, John Taylor, called "the avaricious, monopolizing Spirit of Commerce and Commercial Men." No matter how ludicrous Washington believed Jefferson's monarchical anxieties to be, he could not afford to alienate Virginia. The population of the state—some 750,000 in 1790—was nearly as great as all of New England and half again as large as Pennsylvania. The Union could not survive without Virginia. None of Washington's potential successors could command sufficient respect in Virginia to ensure its continued attachment to the Union. Washington had no choice but to accept a second term and to work to moderate the growing dissension within the government. His election was once again unanimous, but the Republicans demonstrated extraordinary organizational ability and won control of the House of Representatives.[74]

In an effort to build consensus within his divided administration, Washington began to hold frequent meetings with his leading subordinates during his second term. This was the foundation of the cabinet system. Washington had met with his department heads during his first term, but the meetings were less formal and rarely involved all three department heads and the Attorney General. In the cabinet Washington could give both sides a respectful hearing, encourage compromise, and resolve disagreements quickly. During the neutrality crisis that resulted from the outbreak of war between Britain and France in early 1793, the cabinet proved to be an especially efficient and effective device for formulating policy. Washington frequently called for votes in the cabinet, which often frustrated Jefferson, since Henry Knox ("fool that he is," Jefferson complained) almost always voted with Hamilton, and Attorney General Edmund Randolph tried to maintain a neutral position, which Jefferson described as a "half-way system

Washington usually met with his cabinet at his rented residence on Broad Street in Philadelphia, which he occupied from 1790 until 1797. The house was demolished in 1833.

between wrong & right." Washington usually abided by the group's determinations, but he set aside the cabinet's advice often enough to affirm his independence of its judgment. He did not allow the cabinet to become an executive governing council. It remained an advisory body, and as such has served successive presidents for more than two hundred years.

Jefferson had long expressed his intention to resign at the end of Washington's first term, but at Washington's request he put his departure off until the spring or summer. Later he agreed to remain in office until the end of the year. Washington probably reasoned that the opposition posed less of a threat to the government as long as Jefferson remained in the administration. In an effort to maintain the sectional balance among his department heads, Washington replaced him with another Virginian, Edmund Randolph. The cabinet conflict came to a close with Jefferson's departure, but the party conflict within the government continued to intensify.

Washington was convinced that partisan divisions within the government diminished popular respect for federal law—particularly the revenue laws upon which the government depended. Events in western Pennsylvania during the summer of 1794 seemed to verify this conviction. The federal excise tax on whiskey had been unpopular in the area since it was adopted in 1791. Resistance turned to violence in July 1794 when a party of settlers attacked the home of the regional excise inspector. In the weeks that followed insurgents beat and tarred and feathered excise collectors and forced them to resign, robbed the mails, and demolished the stills of men who had paid their taxes. Radical orators urged settlers to resist federal authority, and called for militia to march on the army post at Pittsburgh.

Washington was certain that the insurrection had been incited by the irresponsible and inflammatory rhetoric of the opposition press and orchestrated by the Democratic Societies—popular political associations loosely modeled on the Jacobin clubs of France—that had wide support in western Pennsylvania. There were thirty-five such Democratic Societies across the country by the summer of 1794. Their only purpose, Washington wrote to Henry Lee, was "to sow the seeds of jealousy and distrust among the people, of the government, by destroying all confidence in the Administration of it." If they were not stopped, he told Edmund Randolph, "they will destroy the government."[75]

Washington was determined to demonstrate that the federal government possessed the ability and the will to uphold the law. The alternative, as he saw it, was a rapid descent into anarchy and confusion. On August 7, 1794, he issued a proclamation declaring his intention to call out the militia to suppress the insurrection. Before he ordered the militia to march, however, he sent a three-man commission to the region to give the opposition leaders a final opportunity to submit to the law. When the commissioners presented an unfavorable report, Washington ordered the militia to march. He rode at the head of the army as far as Bedford, Pennsylvania, before turning the command over to Henry Lee and returning to Philadelphia. The army reached the Pittsburgh area at the end of October, but by that time the insurrection had vanished. Hundreds of people were rounded up and questioned. Twenty were ultimately arrested and taken to Philadelphia, but of these, only two were convicted of treason. Washington pardoned them both.

Critics then and since have described Washington's response to the unrest in western Pennsylvania as completely disproportionate. Republicans interpreted the episode as a part of Hamilton's plot to use Washington's authority to subvert the Constitution. "An insurrection was announced and proclaimed and armed against, but could never be found," Jefferson wrote to James Monroe, "& all this under the sanction of a name which has done too much good not to be sufficient to cover harm also." But most Americans applauded the combination of energetic determination and forbearance that characterized Washington's conduct in dealing with the rebellion. "He was anxious to prevent bloodshed," conceded William Findley, a Republican congressman from western Pennsylvania who was involved in the uprising, "and at the same time to enforce due submission to the laws."[76]

The suppression of the Whiskey Rebellion demonstrated that the federal government was willing and able to enforce compliance with federal law, fixing a limit beyond which partisan opposition would not be permitted to go. But in the long term it did little to discourage partisan conflict. In his annual message to Congress delivered in November 1794, Washington blamed the insurrection on "certain self-created societies"—an allusion to the Democratic Societies—and almost all of them were quickly dissolved by their members. But opponents of the administration scarcely paused in their efforts to rally popular sentiment. Indeed the opposition press became bolder in the months after the rebellion, and began charging that Washington had become the tool of Hamilton and his corrupt faction. Scurrilous writers even attacked Washington's character and motives, charging that he was a British agent, a womanizer, a miser, and a notorious blasphemer.

Few things in the last years of his administration troubled Washington more deeply than these attacks on his character, unless it was the charge that he had ceased to be the patriot leader of the whole nation and had become a mere partisan at last. He could hardly have imagined, he wrote to Jefferson in the summer of 1796, "that while I was using my utmost exertions to establish a national character of our own" that "every act of my administration would be tortured, and the grossest, most insidious mis-representations of them be made . . . in such exaggerated and indecent terms as could scarcely be applied to a Nero; a notorious defaulter; or even to a common pickpocket." His public career, he insisted to Jefferson, supplied "abundant proof" that "I was no party man myself, and the first wish of my heart was, if parties did exist, to reconcile them."[77]

Washington regarded the development of partisan divisions in the federal government as one of the greatest disappointments of his presidency. He had hoped that the establishment of the new government under the Federal Constitution would signal the beginning of an era of republican unity, free of the divisive spirit of partisanship. But he grasped at an illusion. Party, faction, schism, lawlessness, and rebellion had marked American life since before the Revolutionary War. The dislocation of traditional authority during the Revolution presented countless opportunities for groups to redress grievances or take advantage of new circumstances to contest for a share of political power. The revolutionary ideal of popular sovereignty, the large-scale mobilization of ordinary people to take part in the Revolutionary War, and the remarkable increase in the number of newspapers stimulated popular participation in political life to a degree that startled everyone. The years between the end of the war and the establishment of the government under the Federal Constitution had been marked by an unprecedented amount of popular political activity, much of it intensely partisan. Through all of this Washington had lived and in much of it he had taken part. His stubborn determination to banish political parties from public life was based on the purest motives, but it reflected little of his usual astute assessment of reality.

Washington's hostility to political parties looked backward, in part, to a society founded on deference to the leadership of gentlemen like himself. Like most of the gentry leaders of his generation, Washington was unable to distinguish between opposition to the policies of the government and opposition to the government itself. Washington was perhaps more blind to this distinction than most, because he had invested so much of himself in the success of the federal government. But Washington's frustration with partisanship was also based on the revolutionary ideal of an informed citizenry making its own choices without any formal institutions—like the "self-created societies" he condemned so vehemently—pretending to mediate between the people and their representatives. He regarded parties, not as vehicles for the expression of popular sovereignty, but as agencies that would subvert the sovereignty of the people by illegitimately claiming to speak on their behalf while actually expressing the views of a factious minority.

The development of political parties filled Washington with dread for the future of the Union. But by refusing to choose openly between the contending parties, and working to reconcile their leaders, Washington established the principle that the president should stand above party, and represent all of the people. This principle, though often compromised and sometimes ignored, remains one of the defining ideals of the American presidency.

CHAPTER SIX

THE NATIONAL INTEREST

GEORGE WASHINGTON ASSUMED THE PRESIDENCY ON the eve of one of the greatest international crises of modern history. Within a few months of Washington's inauguration, the fall of the Bastille to a Parisian mob signaled the beginning of the French Revolution. The Revolution began as an internal event, but quickly developed into an ideological struggle pitting the militant modern republicanism of France against the united monarchies of Europe in a conflict that shook the European state system to its foundations. This ideological struggle plunged Europe into a series of wars that continued with few interruptions until 1815. The principles of universal equality and the rights of man enunciated so forcefully by the French revolutionaries resonated throughout the Atlantic world.

The United States was drawn irresistibly into this crisis. Americans had established the world's first modern republic, and many Americans felt an ideological kinship with the French revolutionaries, whose political aspirations seemed to mirror their own. This sentiment was reinforced by gratitude for French assistance in establishing American independence, and the resulting sense that the United States should support republican France in its struggle for survival against the corrupt and degenerate monarchies of Europe. The wars precipitated by the French Revolution involved nearly every country in Europe, including all of the colonial powers with interests in the New World. The conflict pitted the world's greatest maritime powers—Great Britain and France—in a death struggle in which each nation sought to deny the benefits of American commerce to the other, without regard for American independence or neutral rights. Despite the distance that separated the United States from the Old World, the American alliance with France and antipathy to Britain carried the new nation inexorably

Key to the Bastille. *The key to the Bastille, sent to Washington by Lafayette, is a physical reminder of Washington's stature as a revolutionary leader and the international turmoil that marked his presidency.*

toward war. Among George Washington's most important accomplishments as president was keeping the United States out of the European war, giving the new nation an opportunity to prosper and grow in strength, while establishing the principle of American neutrality with regard to the conflicts of Europe that shaped American foreign policy for more than a century.

Like most Americans, Washington welcomed the first stages of the French Revolution as evidence that the contagion of liberty unleashed in the American Revolution had spread to the Old World. "The American Revolution," Washington proudly wrote to Michel St. Jean de Crévecoeur, "seems to have opened the eyes of almost every nation in Europe, and a spirit of equal liberty appears fast to be gaining ground everywhere, which must afford peculiar satisfaction to every friend of mankind." A few months after the fall of the Bastille, Lafayette sent Washington the main key to the prison as "a tribute Which I owe to you, as A Son to My Adoptive father, as an aide de Camp to My General, as a Missionary of liberty to its patriarch." When he received the key in New York in August 1790, the President sent Lafayette his sincere thanks for this "token of victory gained by Liberty over Despotism." Washington displayed the relic in his presidential homes in New York and Philadelphia. Shortly before his retirement he sent it back to Mount Vernon, where it was placed in the main passage (the most public part of the house) in what a visitor described as a "kind of small crystal lantern."[78]

Despite his early enthusiasm, Washington observed events in France with a caution shared by few of his countrymen. Many Americans regarded the dramatic events of 1789—the fall of the Bastille, the formation of the Constituent Assembly, and the promulgation of the Declaration of the Rights of Man and the Citizen—as the crowning achievements of a nearly bloodless revolution. But Washington saw that France had experienced just "the first paroxysm." The Revolution, he wrote, "is of too great magnitude to be effected in so short a space and with the loss of so little blood. The mortification of the King, the intrigues of the Queen, and the discontent of the Princes and the Noblesse will foment divisions, if possible, in the National Assembly, and avail themselves of every faux pas in the formation of the constitution." Washington predicted that "popular licentiousness" on one side and excessive force on the other would alienate the friends of reform. "Great temperance, firmness, and foresight are necessary," he added. "To forebear running from one extreme to another is no easy matter."[79]

Washington's skepticism was reinforced by the reports he received from his own informal agent in Europe, Gouverneur Morris. An urbane New Yorker, Morris was brilliant, self-assured, and possessed of a marvelous sense of humor. Morris also had a scandalous reputation—he had lost a leg in a carriage accident, but the rumor went round that he lost it as the result of an injury sustained in jumping from a married woman's bedroom window. Scandalous or not, Washington thought highly of Morris, and at the outset of his administration asked him to serve as a secret, unofficial emissary to sound out the British government about resolving outstanding disputes and negotiating a commercial treaty with the United States. The mission came to nothing, and Morris moved on to Paris. He quickly charmed his way into the highest circles of French society, assessed the contending political factions, and reported his conclusions to Washington.

Everything Morris wrote suggested events were moving in a radical direction. The king and his ministers meant well, Morris reported, but they meant it "very feebly." Morris found the nobility corrupt and irresponsible, desperate to hold on to its ancient privileges regardless of the circumstances. The moderates in the National Assembly, he wrote to Washington in January 1790, were impractical men who "acquired their ideas of Government from Books." Their systems of government would be "fit for nothing but to be put into Books again." Extremists, he warned, were most numerous and most likely to take control of events. He predicted that a general European war would break out because all sides wanted it—the monarchists in order to put a disciplined military force in the hands of the government with which to suppress the Revolution, radicals in order to impose "Measures of a very decisive Nature" that would never be accepted without a national crisis, the aristocrats "to reestablish that Species of Despotism most suited to their own Cupidity."[80]

In December 1791 Washington named Morris the new United States minister to France. Morris reported faithfully to Washington on the major events of 1792—the attack on the Tuileries, the abolition of the monarchy, the collapse of the first revolutionary constitution, the September Massacres—events that signaled the radicalization of the French Revolution and seemed to verify Morris's predictions. These events turned the French Revolution into an international movement, a revolution without borders in which the French Republic declared itself ready to offer "aid and fraternity to all peoples wishing to recover their liberties" by overthrowing their existing governments. On January 21, 1793, the revolutionary government executed Louis XVI, and a few days later, declared war on Great Britain and the Netherlands. France declared war on Spain shortly thereafter.

The outbreak of a general war forced the European crisis to the center of American politics, where it remained for the remainder of the Washington presidency. American popular sympathies were with the French. France had raised the standard of republicanism and was facing the combined power of Europe's monarchies, which seemed intent on sweeping the republican ideal from the world. Though only a tiny number of Americans seem to have believed that the United States should join the war on the side of the French Republic, many Americans were prepared to do almost anything short of war to assist France in its struggle against the British. The ideological dimensions of the European conflict exacerbated the division within Washington's cabinet and fueled the growing partisan divide between Federalists and Republicans. The European war touched the lives of nearly all Americans in some way, and effected most of the major decisions of Washington's second term.

When news of the outbreak of war reached the United States, Washington and his department heads were in general agreement that the United States should pursue a neutral course. But that broad consensus did not disguise fundamental differences about foreign policy. Thomas Jefferson was reluctant to issue a declaration of neutrality, arguing that the President possessed no such constitutional authority. He also contended that American neutrality "was a thing worth something to the powers at war" and "that they should bid for it." Jefferson wanted to use neutrality as a bargaining point with which to extract commercial concessions from one or the other of the belligerents. Alexander Hamilton, who wanted to avoid antagonizing Britain, held that this was absurd, that the United States was not in a position to take sides in the European conflict and that to attempt to use neutrality as a diplomatic tool would risk war with the British.[81]

Jefferson was ideologically dedicated to the success of the French Revolution. He had observed its early stages firsthand as minister to France, and had concluded in 1788 that "this country will within two or three years be in enjoiment of a tolerably free constitution, and that without its having cost them a drop of blood." Though this prediction turned out to be wrong, the eventual blood-letting did not disturb Jefferson greatly. Rather than see the Revolution fail, he wrote on

January 3, 1793, "I would have seen half the earth desolated. Were there but an Adam & an Eve left in every country, & left free, it would be better than as it now is." But his position at this juncture had more to do with partisan politics than ideological commitments, however much the two were interwoven. The Republican opposition, which was excoriating the monarchical tendencies of Hamilton's financial program, was the political beneficiary of the general enthusiasm for the French Revolution. Jefferson wanted to maintain this enthusiasm and while maintaining enough of the appearance of neutrality to prevent war with Great Britain. A fair neutrality, Jefferson confessed to Madison, would "prove a disagreeable pill to our friends."[82]

Hamilton was skeptical about the outcome of the French Revolution, and his sympathies for its aims turned to intense ideological hostility as the Revolution took a radical turn. He did not expect France to remain a republic for long, anticipating that internal chaos would lead to a military dictatorship or a restoration of the monarchy. War with Great Britain would destroy his carefully constructed financial system, which depended on British trade for revenue. Hamilton wrote that "if we can avoid war for ten or twelve years more, we shall then have acquired a maturity, which will make it no more than a common calamity." Yet to avoid war with Britain, Hamilton was prepared to compromise faithful adherence to the nation's treaty obligations to France. He argued that given the prevailing disorder in France, the United States could treat the alliance of 1778 as temporarily suspended. Neither Jefferson nor Hamilton, in short, actually wanted the United States to be truly neutral. Each wanted to use neutrality as a cover for supporting one side in the ideological struggle.

The ideological dimensions of the European crisis did not particularly concern Washington. A pragmatist in an age of ideological enthusiasm, Washington believed that the parties to the European war were pursuing their national interests, and that in dealing with them, the United States should consult its own interest. Yet Washington was surrounded by men who believed that ideological considerations should take precedence in international relations, including many charmed by the idea that the French Revolution marked an end to the old system of predatory power relations between the states of Europe and initiated a new era in which the enlightened ideals of universal human rights would increasingly shape the policies of nations. No man had devoted himself more completely to the republican ideals of the American Revolution than Washington, but he denied that the self-effacing idealism of republican ideology had any place in foreign relations. "It is a maxim founded on the universal experience of mankind," he wrote, "that no nation is to be trusted farther than it is bound by its interest; and no prudent statesman or politician will venture to depart from it."[83]

Washington was certain that under the circumstances the national interest of the United States dictated a policy of genuine neutrality. War would be disastrous for American commerce and would debilitate the government by shattering the nation's finances. Yet Washington did not believe, as some Americans did, that the national interest dictated a policy of isolation. Washington believed that the United States should avoid becoming involved in European power struggles, but that Americans should cultivate a profitable commercial relationship with Europe. "I hope," Washington had written in 1788, "that the United States of America will be able to keep disengaged from the labyrinth of European politics and war. It should be the policy of the United States to administer to their wants, without being engaged in their quarrels."[84]

Neither Hamilton nor Jefferson really shared Washington's vision of a truly independent United States pursuing its own interest without reference to European power politics or the ideological conflict raging in Europe. Both men believed that the fate of the United States depended on which side won the European war, and engaged in private intrigues to ensure the United States came out on the winning side. Jefferson confided in a series of French emissaries, and pretended not to notice their clandestine efforts to make the United States an outpost of France. Hamilton passed privileged information to a British agent, George Beckwith, whom he thought was giving him privileged information in return, and later befriended the British minister, George Hammond, whom Jefferson studiously snubbed. The indiscretions of Jefferson's successor as Secretary of State, Edmund Randolph, with the French ambassador cost Randolph his job and blackened his reputation, but they were different only in degree. Washington understood, as few of his contemporaries did, that these petty court intrigues only diminished the United States in the eyes of Europeans.

Washington recognized that the success of the French Revolution might inaugurate a new system in international affairs that would probably benefit the United States, but unlike his chief subordinates, Washington did not believe that the outcome of the European wars was vital to the future of the nation. The future of the United States, in Washington's view, depended on the increase in American wealth and economic opportunity that would come with the growth of commerce and westward expansion. He was determined to establish the "national character" of the United States, distinct from that of any European nation.

Regardless of Washington's determination, a genuine neutrality was hard to maintain. American neutrality was already compromised by the terms of the Franco-American Alliance of 1778, which bound the United States to defend France's West Indian possessions against aggressors. Britain's naval superiority made a British attack on the French islands almost certain. Moreover, the Franco-American Treaty of Amity and Commerce of 1778 granted France the right to bring prizes into American ports, while the enemies of France were forbidden to arm or provision their vessels in the United States.

The cabinet debate over the nation's obligations to France under the treaties was spirited, and the details of the Neutrality Proclamation issued on April 22, 1793, and the policies devised in the following months to maintain American neutrality reflected ideas of both Hamilton and Jefferson. At Jefferson's suggestion, the word "neutrality" did not appear in the proclamation, but the sense of the document was clear. The proclamation pledged the United States to pursue "conduct friendly and impartial toward the belligerent powers" and forbid American citizens from aiding the warring powers within the boundaries of the United States. The decision to issue the proclamation—which was ultimately Washington's alone—set an important constitutional precedent, asserting the initiative of the executive branch in foreign affairs.

The proclamation was one of the most controversial acts of the Washington presidency, and exposed Washington to charges that he was hostile to France and had overstepped his constitutional authority. Some of the worst attacks came from Freneau's *National Gazette*. At one cabinet meeting, Washington exploded at the charges being made by "that rascal Freneau." According to Jefferson's account of the event, Washington angrily "defied any man on earth to produce one single act of his since he had been in the government which was not done on the purest motives." He said that "he had rather be in his grave than in his present situation. That he had rather be on his farm than be made emperor of the world and yet they were charging him with wanting to be king."[85]

The hostility of the opposition press to Washington stood in stark contrast to the popular enthusiasm for the new ambassador of the French Republic, Edmond Genet, who arrived in Philadelphia on May

16, 1793 after a triumphal overland journey from Charleston, South Carolina. Genet's mission presented the first challenge to Washington's neutrality policy. Genet was young, handsome, and filled with revolutionary fervor. His main goal was to ensure the flow of American grain to France, but he was also instructed to encourage the people of Canada, Florida, and Louisiana to throw off their colonial oppressors, assist American citizens to invade Spanish territory, and recruit American privateers to prey on British and Spanish shipping. He was also directed to negotiate a new treaty with the United States in which the two republics mutually pledged "to assist in every way the extension of the empire of liberty, guarantee the sovereignty of peoples, and punish the powers that still hold to an exclusive colonial and commercial system, by declaring that the vessels of those powers shall not be admitted to the ports of the two contracting nations." To pay all of the expenses he incurred in spreading French principles of universal liberty in the New World, Genet was to seek the immediate liquidation of the United States debt to France—about $5.6 million.[86]

In short, Genet's mission was to make the United States an outpost of militant French republicanism, and to get the American government to pay for the privilege. The entire program was a tissue of absurdities, because the moment the United States involved itself in the sort of belligerent activities Genet was sent to encourage, its shipping would be swept from the seas by the British Navy, and the revenues out of which the United States might have paid the debt to France would evaporate. Genet seems never to have grasped this reality, and persisted in his mission until it collapsed under the weight of its own internal contradictions and the shift in popular opinion against him.

Washington received Genet with courteous reserve two days after the minister arrived in Philadelphia, and treated his various overtures to the government with cold formality. Washington and his cabinet quickly agreed that the government should decline Genet's request for advance payment of the debt. This effectively ended any possibility that Genet would be able to execute most of his grand design, although he showed no sign of recognizing this fact. He had already begun dispatching privateers from American ports, recruiting American citizens (including Revolutionary War hero George Rogers Clark) to carry out expeditions against British and Spanish possessions, and committed other violations of American neutrality that threatened to involve the United States in the European war.

Genet miscalculated that popular enthusiasm for his mission would ultimately force Washington to tolerate his schemes, though he complained that "Old Washington impedes my course in a thousand ways." But he misunderstood the enormous trust the people had in Washington. On June 22 Genet presented Jefferson with a letter protesting the unfriendly response accorded him by Washington, which he insisted was utterly inconsistent with the will of the people. That will, Genet predicted, would be reflected by very different policies Congress would adopt when it met in December. Hamilton described the letter as "the most offensive paper, perhaps, that ever was offered by a foreign Minister to a friendly power, with which he resided."[87]

Washington shrewdly allowed popular enthusiasm for Genet to spend itself before acting to suppress his activities—giving the impetuous minister an opportunity to commit transgressions against American neutrality so flagrant that even his supporters would begin to turn away from him. Washington was confident enough that Genet would be the instrument of his own undoing that he left Philadelphia and went to Mount Vernon. Within days he learned that Genet permitted a newly outfitted privateer to sail from Philadelphia in defiance of presidential orders, and had threatened to take an appeal directly to the American people over the President's head. "Is the Minister of the French Republic to set the Act of this Government at defiance, with impunity?" Washington demanded, "and then threaten the Executive with an appeal to the People? What must the world think of such conduct, and of the Government of the United States in submitting to it?"

A message was shortly thereafter sent to Paris demanding Genet's recall. Public meetings in cities from Boston to Richmond condemned Genet and expressed support for Washington and the neutrality policy. The new French minister who arrived with Genet's recall in February 1794 also carried orders to arrest Genet and return him to France for trial, a path that could only have ended at the guillotine. Washington generously granted Genet asylum. He became a citizen of the United States, married Cornelia Clinton, the daughter of Gov. George Clinton of New York, and lived quietly on a farm near Albany until his death in 1834.

The Genet affair impressed upon Washington and his subordinates the need to define the rules governing the conduct of belligerents in American ports and the terms of American neutrality more generally. They agreed to forbid the arming of foreign ships in American ports, defined American territorial waters, denied foreign consuls the authority

With plain dress, simple habits, and strict attention to the constitutional limits of his office, Washington set an example of republican leadership admired throughout the Western World.

to conduct prize courts in American territory. These and other principles worked out within the administration during the last months of 1793 were embodied in the Neutrality Act passed by Congress in

1794. These principles, formulated by Washington and his subordinates under the pressure of events, constituted a system of such comprehensive precision that it served the needs of American diplomacy until the First World War.

The recall of Genet did not end the threats to American neutrality. During the months that Washington and his subordinates were struggling to prevent Genet from drawing the United States into war, relations with Britain were steadily degenerating. The British were determined to prevent American grain and other provisions from reaching France, and were not inclined to respect American neutral rights in doing so. In June 1793 the British government authorized its navy to detain all vessels carrying foodstuffs to France, and scores of American ships were stopped and their cargoes confiscated. Hamilton, fearing that the United States was moving closer to war with Britain, discouraged Washington from taking actions that would exacerbate the crisis. Washington, recognizing the importance of asserting American neutral rights, was unmoved. He laid the matter before Congress in December 1793, and shortly after the new year Congress began considering Thomas Jefferson's long-cherished proposals to discriminate against trade with Britain.[88]

Within a few weeks, new provocations by the British pushed the United States to the verge of war. In March 1794 word reached Philadelphia that the British government had ordered its navy to seize any ship bound for the French West Indies, or even suspected of trading with the French colonies. As a result of this order, hundreds of American ships were confiscated by British warships cruising in the Caribbean. Shortly after receiving this news, Washington learned that Lord Dorchester, the governor of Canada, had delivered an inflammatory speech to the hostile Indians predicting the outbreak of war between the United States and Britain.

Washington was prepared to take any step consistent with national honor to preserve peace, but the role he should assume in this crisis was not clearly evident. In the spring of 1793 Washington had assumed, over Jefferson's opposition, that the President possessed the authority to proclaim American neutrality without the consent of Congress, which was not in session. But Congress had since convened, and as the nation faced a choice between war and peace—a choice constitutionality reserved to Congress—it was not clear that the initiative lay with the President. Congress and the cabinet were divided, both on this question and the more substantive one of how to respond to the British. In the face of all of this uncertainty, Washington seized the initiative and assumed responsibility for resolving the crisis, establishing a precedent that defined the president as the unrivaled leader of American foreign policy.

Federalist senators, anxious to avoid war, urged Washington to send Alexander Hamilton on a mission to London to negotiate a comprehensive settlement. Washington believed this plan invited national humiliation. Hamilton would never do in any case, Washington told the leader of the delegation, because he "did not possess the general confidence of the country."[89] But shortly thereafter the President received word that the offending British orders had been revoked. A few days later Washington received a dispatch from the American minister in London, Thomas Pinckney, conveying assurances from the British government that the orders had been temporary and that most of the vessels seized by the British Navy would not be condemned. This was hardly an apology, but it revealed the potential for a negotiated settlement. After a series of private consultations, Washington named Chief Justice John Jay to negotiate a treaty with the British.

Washington's course was unpopular. A large part of the population was howling for war. The Republicans, led principally by Madison since Jefferson had retired to Monticello, charged that Washington had usurped the legitimate role of Congress and violated the constitutional separation of powers by appointing the Chief Justice to negotiate a treaty that would result in judicial proceedings over which he would preside. The criticism galled Washington, but he recognized this as the crisis for which he had husbanded his reputation so carefully for so long. Jay arrived in England on June 12, 1794. His negotiations with the British Secretary of State for Foreign Affairs, William Wyndham, Lord Grenville, lasted until November 19, 1794, when the two signed a convention known since as Jay's Treaty. It was the first foreign treaty negotiated by the United States government under the Federal Constitution, and one of the most controversial treaties in American history.

The text of the treaty did not reach Washington until March, 1795. Jay had obtained much of what he was sent for—the evacuation of the western posts, compensation for the seizure of American ships, and the admission of American ships of no more than seventy tons to the British West Indies. In return he had renounced the imposition of discriminatory duties on British shipping and the sequestration of debts owed to British creditors. But Grenville had refused to admit the sort of neutral trading rights that Americans claimed, and the treaty said nothing about the impressment of American seamen by the British Navy. Jay had also not been able to persuade the British to compensate Americans for slaves freed or carried off by British troops during the Revolutionary War. A solution to this problem would have been hard to devise, and Jay—who was opposed to slavery—had not tried very hard. Jay had made only one important mistake. In order to persuade Grenville to allow Americans limited access to the British West Indies, he agreed that Americans would not export certain tropical products— sugar, molasses, cocoa, coffee, and cotton—that the British wanted to transport to Europe in their own ships. This was a major blunder, because Americans carried most of the products of the French islands to Europe, and cotton was becoming an important crop in the United States itself.

Washington decided to sign the treaty if the Senate approved it at a special session in June. The text remained a secret until that time. The Senate divided along partisan lines: the twenty Federalist senators for the treaty, the ten Republicans against. But the Senate insisted on expunging the offending article on the re-export trade, and Washington was not certain that the Constitution authorized him to sign a treaty under these circumstances. His uncertainty was compounded by the popular reaction to the treaty. When the treaty was finally published in July, Jay was burned in effigy all over the nation. Jay's failure to secure compensation for lost slaves and his pledge to honor debts due to British creditors (owed mainly by southerners) infuriated southern planters. Hamilton was pelted with stones while giving a speech in favor of the treaty, and public demonstrations condemning the treaty were staged by Republicans in cities and towns all over the North.

Washington regarded these protests as senseless. The "cry against the Treaty is like that against a mad-dog," he complained to Hamilton. But in the midst of these protests Washington learned that the British Navy had resumed taking American ships carrying grain to France. This fresh provocation prompted Washington to delay ratification for several weeks, but he ultimately signed the treaty on August 14, 1795. The treaty was the price Washington paid for a peace he believed was indispensable for the survival of the American nation.[90]

Popular sentiment, so violently against the treaty in the spring and summer, swung the other way in the fall of 1795. The shift was undoubtedly prompted by a combination of factors—public meetings and petitions expressing support for the treaty, Alexander Hamilton's exhaustive series of newspaper essays, and the timely announcement of Anthony Wayne's treaty with the northwestern Indians—but at bottom the change was probably a response to the profound confidence most Americans had in Washington's judgment.

The Republican leadership in the House of Representatives made a final effort to block the treaty at the beginning of 1796 by refusing to vote the funds necessary to put it into effect. This debate, Washington wrote, brought the Federal Constitution "to the brink of a precipice." He viewed the attempt of Republican leaders in the House to direct foreign policy through the power of the purse as a subversion of the Constitution, which entrusted treaty making to the president and the Senate. The House leadership demanded Washington turn over Jay's instructions and other documents related to his mission. Washington refused, informing the House that it had no constitutional right to any of the papers unless it was considering his impeachment. Washington's scorn and increasing popular pressure caused the opposition to wither. On April 30, 1796, the House of Representatives approved the funds necessary to implement Jay's Treaty by a vote of 51 to 48. Washington regarded this victory as one of the most important events in the short history of the republic.

Washington envisioned neutrality as a policy that would ensure American prosperity over the long term, but its wisdom was evident almost immediately. The upheaval in Europe generated an insatiable demand for American goods, particularly grain, and created an unprecedented opportunity for American merchants, whose ships constituted the largest fleet of neutral vessels in the world. When Washington assumed the presidency, about half of all American overseas trade was carried in American ships. By the time he left office, this number had risen to almost ninety-five percent. The net profits of American overseas merchants rose during the same period from about five million dollars a year to well over twenty million dollars a year. Shipbuilding boomed, and with it, the demand for lumber, rope, canvas, and tar. So did the demand for labor. Wages in the major port cities more than doubled during the Washington administration. The boom rippled outward to the commercial farms in the hinterland, where profits and wages rose. The new prosperity was most dramatically reflected in the increase in the amount of consumer goods imported from Great Britain. Although import prices remained fairly stable, the volume of imports soared, doubling between 1794 and 1795. Ordinary

Americans indulged themselves in goods that had once been reserved for the homes of the wealthy—fine fabrics, lace curtains, Staffordshire china, carpets, and other luxuries.[91]

George Washington was not responsible for this extraordinary boom in the American economy. But he foresaw the economic advantages that would flow from a policy of neutrality more clearly than most of his contemporaries, and worked tirelessly to keep the United States out of the European war and free of foreign entanglements that would have endangered American independence. His highest aim, he explained to Patrick Henry in the fall of 1795, was "the dignity, happiness, and true interest of the people of this country. My ardent desire is, and my aim has been . . . to comply strictly with all our engagements, foreign and domestic, but to keep the United States free from political connexions with every other Country. To see that they may be independent of all, and under the influence of none. In a word, I want an American character, that the powers of Europe may be convinced we act for ourselves and not for others; this in my judgement, is the only way to be respected abroad and happy at home and not by becoming partizans of Great Britain or France," which could only "create dissensions, disturb the public tranquility, and destroy, perhaps for ever the cement which binds the Union."[92]

Epilogue
A Final Farewell

GEORGE WASHINGTON IS GENERALLY CREDITED WITH establishing a precedent that no President should serve more than two terms, a principle embodied in the Federal Constitution by the ratification of the 22nd Amendment in 1951. But the precedent was a wholly accidental one. Even before he assumed office in 1789, Washington privately indicated that he intended to step down "as soon as my services could possibly with propriety be dispensed with."[93] He apparently contemplated resigning from office during his first term, and accepted re-election in 1792 with great reluctance after wrestling with the decision for several months. By the beginning of 1796, if not long before, he was disgusted with public life. There is no evidence that he considered a third term. But nowhere in his surviving papers did Washington suggest that he believed no president should serve more than two terms.

In the spring of 1792, when he was anticipating retirement at the end of his first term, Washington enlisted James Madison to assist him to prepare a message suitable for the occasion—conveying his determination not to be a candidate for re-election, but more importantly offering some final advice to the people of the United States. Washington saved Madison's draft after he accepted a second term. This draft served as the basis for what became known as Washington's "Farewell Address." In early 1796 Washington prepared a new draft and sent it to Alexander Hamilton for suggestions and revisions. Hamilton returned two revised drafts. Washington preferred the first, and after making final revisions of his own, delivered the message to the editor of the Philadelphia *American Daily Advertiser*. It was published on September 19, 1796. Early that same morning, Washington rode out of Philadelphia headed for Mount Vernon, to place himself beyond any appeal that he reconsider.

The Upper Garden at Mount Vernon. Washington returned to Mount Vernon in spring of 1797, hoping to spend his final years in quiet retirement, tending his gardens and improving his estate.

Others called the message Washington's "Farewell Address." He gave it no title at all, starting simply with the salutation "Friends and fellow Citizens," signaling his intention to address the American people directly. Washington's first purpose was to announce that he would not accept another term as president. Had Washington not spoken out, his reelection—despite the partisan controversies of his second term—was certain. But taking his reelection for granted would have been immodest. As early as 1792 Washington had pondered how to decline another term without being guilty of the arrogance implicit in presuming that he would be chosen. In the Farewell Address, he tactfully announced his decision "to decline being numbered among those, out of whom a choice is to be made" at the upcoming election. Washington explained that his service as president had always involved "a uniform sacrifice of inclination to the opinion of duty," but that duty did not seem to demand that he continue in office any longer.[94]

Having announced his decision, Washington moved on to the broader purpose of the address—"to offer to your solemn contemplation, and to recommend to your frequent review, some sentiments; which are the result of much reflection, of no inconsiderable observation, and which appear to me all important to the permanency of your felicity as a people." These reflections constitute Washington's most sustained attempt to convey the political lessons he had learned during a life almost entirely expended in the service of his country.

The higher purpose of the United States, Washington explained, was to demonstrate to mankind the practicality of self-government, thus recommending that system to "the applause, the affection, and adoption of every nation which is yet a stranger to it." This could only be accomplished if the United States remained united and independent of foreign influence, and established a national character distinct from that of any country in Europe. Washington called on Americans of all sections and political persuasions to set aside their local loyalties, partisan sentiments, and partiality for any foreign state in order to establish the national character of the United States. He advised his fellow citizens to cherish the Union and to observe good faith and justice towards all nations, and warned them against political partisanship, foreign influence in politics, and foreign policies that involved the United States in the political affairs of Europe.

The Union, Washington insisted, "is the main Pillar in the Edifice of your real independence, the support of your tranquility at home; your peace abroad; of your safety; of your prosperity; of that very Liberty which you so highly prize." The Union was based on the sentimental bond between Americans—a bond founded on common trials, religious principles, manners, habits, and political ideas. But Washington grounded his argument for cherishing the Union on a hard-headed assessment of the interests of citizens of the different states. To those who continued to argue against the practicality of a continental republic, Washington contended that the different parts of the nation benefit from commercial interaction with one another. Together they possessed greater strength, greater resources and greater security from external forces than they did alone. Together they would prosper and grow in strength.

The greatest danger to the Union, Washington warned, was the divisive spirit of partisanship. Partisan divisions were senseless, he contended, because with "slight shades of difference," Americans "have the same religion, manners, habits, and political principles." He admitted that parties might sometimes offer "useful checks upon the Administration of the Government," but contended that there would always be enough of this kind of vigilance in popular governments without parties. In opposition to those who sought to make "the public administration the mirror of the ill-concerted and incongruous projects of faction," Washington posed the ideal of a unified public good that would transcend the petty differences and narrow selfish interests that typically divided men. He appealed to his fellow citizens to give up their suspicions of government and to lend their support to "consistent and wholesome plans, digested by common counsels and modified by mutual interests."

Washington urged the national interest as the only sensible foundation for foreign relations. Passionate aversion or attachment to any foreign nation, he warned, would blind Americans to their true interest. Passionate attachment to any foreign nation "facilitate the illusion of an imaginary common interest, in cases where no real common interest exists." Such attachments would also lead "Ambitious, corrupted, or deluded citizens" to "betray, or sacrifice the interests of their own country" and expose the nation to the intrigues of foreign agents. Washington was undoubtedly thinking of Britain and France, but he did not name either nation. His purpose was to establish general principles that would be useful to Americans for generations.

If the United States scrupulously adhered to its own interest, Washington predicted, it would soon become strong enough to defy any foreign threat and to "choose peace or war, as our interest, guided by our justice shall Counsel." It was the interest of the United States, Washington contended, to have "as little political connection" with Europe as possible. He advised Americans to "steer clear of permanent alliances." Nowhere in the address did Washington use the phrase "entangling alliances" often attributed to him—the phrase was used by Jefferson in his First Inaugural Address. Washington did not object to "temporary alliances for extraordinary emergencies." But he insisted that Americans should not "entangle our peace and prosperity in the toils of European Ambition, Rivalship, Interest, Humour or Caprice."

Washington's Farewell Address is justly remembered as one of the greatest American state papers, aptly described by two recent commentators as the "most complete articulation of his project to create a modern, self-sufficient American political community—in the form of a large commercial republic—able to command its own fortunes through a foreign policy that pursued American interest, guided by justice."[95]

The address was quickly reprinted in newspapers and pamphlets all over the United States and was republished in Europe. Federalists acclaimed it as a monument of statecraft. "The advice he gives to the nation," Philadelphian Jacob Hiltzheimer wrote, "I hope will be remembered by all good citizens to the end of time." Federalists also saw the political implications of the address and Washington's decision not to serve another term. "It will serve as a signal," Congressman Fisher Ames wrote, "to the party racers to start, and I expect a great deal of noise, whipping, and spurring."[96]

Republicans charged that the Farewell Address was a campaign document aimed at the election of a Federalist president. James Madison claimed that the address was hostile toward the French, and demonstrated that Washington "is completely in the snares of the British faction." Republicans also charged that Washington waited until September to decline another term to prevent them from mounting a sustained challenge to Vice President John Adams, Washington's most obvious Federalist successor. When the electoral votes were counted, Adams held an advantage of only three votes over his closest rival, Thomas Jefferson. Under the electoral system then in use, Adams became president and Jefferson became vice president.[97]

On Saturday, March 4, 1797, Washington put on his best black velvet suit, dispensed with his aristocratic coach, and walked to the State House for John Adams' inauguration. Inside he took his seat on the dais and listened attentively while the president-elect delivered his

Inaugural Address and took the oath of office. "A solemn scene it was indeed," Adams reported to his wife, Abigail, "and it was made affecting to me by the presence of the General, whose countenance was as serene and unclouded as the day." Most of the spectators, Adams wrote, were in tears over the imminent departure of Washington. When the participants rose to leave the hall, Washington—a private citizen once more—beckoned Vice President Jefferson to precede him. Jefferson hesitated, but Washington gestured again, more insistently, and this time Jefferson complied.

This transition of power from one head of state to another was one of the most remarkable events of Washington's presidency. Throughout the eighteenth-century world, heads of state were normally displaced by death or violence, force or fraud. Washington's final accomplishment as president was surrendering power gracefully to Adams. A smooth transition was essential to demonstrate that a republican people were truly capable of governing themselves, or in Washington's words, "to convince the world that the happiness of nations can be accomplished by pacific revolutions in their political systems, without the destructive intervention of the sword."[98]

The transition seemed almost effortless, but appearances disguised an underlying tension. The relationship between Washington and Adams had long been cool. Before taking office, Washington had expected to make the vice president an active participant in the administration, but at the outset Adams had made himself a political liability by advocating a measure to bestow elaborate titles on federal officials. This proposal made Adams extremely unpopular in Virginia, and Washington subsequently kept him at arms length. Adams had played almost no role in the administration, and Washington probably wondered whether Adams possessed the prudence or executive ability the presidency demands. But any misgivings Washington felt about his successor were overwhelmed by his pleasure at finally being relieved of the burdens of the presidency, and the mixed feelings he had about leaving his friends in Philadelphia and returning to his beloved Mount Vernon. "He seemed to me," Adams wrote the next day, "to enjoy a triumph over me. Methought I heard him say, 'Ay! I am fairly out and you are fairly in! See which of us will be the happiest!'"[99]

After the inauguration ceremony, George Washington walked to the Francis Hotel to call on President Adams. He was followed down Chestnut Street by a crowd of admirers, who watched as the door closed behind the former president. Seconds later Washington came back out, and stood in the doorway, hat in hand, to acknowledge the silent homage of the people. He lingered for a parting moment before he stepped inside and closed the door.[100]

Having forged the powers of the presidency and wielded them with effectiveness for eight years, Washington deserved the homage of his countrymen. He had done more than any other person to maintain the independence of the United States and to secure the tenuous Union of those states. He restored the people's confidence in executive leadership, and set a standard of conduct for national leaders—sometimes dishonored, but never wholly forgotten—that has endured for more than two centuries. He lent his prestige to the establishment of a financial system that rescued the new nation from insolvency and placed it on the road to prosperity, pushed back the western frontier, guided the creation of a capital city that would one day be the envy of the world, and in a time of intense partisanship, gave his office a character that transcends politics. By leading the new nation between the combatants in the general European war, he gave the Union a chance to mature and grow in strength.

Washington envisioned a grand future for the United States, and he worked to realize that vision with resourcefulness, ability, and selfless determination. He asked no less of his fellow citizens. His call to them was meant for us as well: "It should be the highest ambition of every American to extend his views beyond himself, and to bear in mind that his conduct will not only affect himself, his country, and his immediate posterity; but that its influence may be co-extensive with the world, and stamp political happiness or misery on ages yet unborn."[101]

NOTES

PROLOGUE

1. Donald Jackson and Dorothy Twohig, eds., *The Diaries of George Washington*, 6 vols. (Charlottesville, Va., 1976-79), 5: 445.
2. GW to Henry Knox, April 1, 1789, Dorothy Twohig, Mark A. Mastromarino, and Jack D. Warren, Jr., eds., *The Papers of George Washington*, 9 vols. to date (Charlottesville, Va. 1987-2000), [cited hereafter as *PGW*, PS], 2: 2-3.
3. For GW's debt, see GW to Richard Conway, March 4 and 6, 1789, *PGW*, PS 1: 361-62, 368-69. GW discharged the debt, in full with interest, on December 15, 1790. The salaries of the secretaries of state and treasury were initially fixed at $3,500, that of the Secretary of War at $3,000. The first ministers GW sent to London and Paris were paid $9,000 a year each, plus another $9,000 for their "outfit." Alexander Hamilton estimated in 1789 that a gentleman could live in modest comfort in New York City for $1,000 a year (Leonard White, *The Federalists: A Study in Administrative History, 1789-1801* [New York, 1948], 294).
4. GW to Henry Lee, September 22, 1788, W.W. Abbot, ed., *The Papers of George Washington*, Confederation Series, 6 vols. (Charlottesville, Va. 1992-1997), [cited hereafter as *PGW*, CS] 6: 528-31.
5. GW to Henry Lee, September 22, 1788, *PGW*, CS 6: 528-31; GW to James Warren, October 7, 1785, *PGW*, CS 3: 298-301; GW to James Madison, November 5, 1786, *PGW*, CS 4: 331-32.
6. GW to Lafayette, January 29, 1789, *PGW*, PS 1: 262-64.
7. Edmund S. Morgan, *The Genius of George Washington* (Washington, D.C., 1980), 22.
8. GW to Samuel Vaughan, March 21, 1789, *PGW*, PS 1: 424-30; The most thorough account of GW's journey is in Douglas Southall Freeman, *George Washington: Patriot and President* (New York, 1954), 166-84; GW to Edward Rutledge, May 5, 1789, *PGW*, PS 2: 217-18.
9. Fisher Ames to George R. Minot, May 3, 1789, William B. Allen, ed., *The Works of Fisher Ames*, 2 vols. (Indianapolis, 1983), 1: 567-69; First Inaugural Address, *PGW*, PS 2: 173-77.

CHAPTER ONE

10. Pierce Butler to Weedon Butler, May 5, 1788, Max Farrand, ed., *The Records of the Federal Convention of 1787*, 4 vols. (New Haven, Conn., 1937), 3: 301-304; Joseph Gales, comp., *The Debates and Proceedings in the Congress of the United States*, 42 vols. (Washington, D.C., 1834-56), 1: 550-51.
11. GW to Bushrod Washington, July 27 1789, *PGW*, PS 3: 334; Bushrod Washington had written to his uncle in an unsuccessful effort to obtain a federal appointment.
12. GW to David Stuart, June 15, 1790, *PGW*, PS 5: 523-28.
13. GW to Samuel Vaughan, March 21, 1789, *PGW*, PS 1: 424-30.
14. The pioneering study of appointments during GW's presidency, Gallaird Hunt, "Office-Seeking during Washington's Administration," *American Historical Review*, 1 (1896), slightly underestimates the total; GW remains the only president to appoint every member of the Supreme Court.
15. John Adams to Silvanus Bourne, August 30, 1789, Adams Papers, Massachusetts Historical Society.
16. In response to complaints from South Carolinians about being passed over for high federal appointments, Sen. Pierce Butler explained to Gov. Thomas Pinckney that GW felt compelled to nominate John Jay as chief justice instead of South Carolina's John Rutledge because of Jay's former prominence in the Confederation government, which made it "impossible to place him in any secondary station" (Pierce Butler to Thomas Pinckney, December 17, 1789, Pierce Butler Letterbook, Historical Society of Pennsylvania). GW later nominated Rutledge to succeed Jay.
17. This event probably took place on August 5, 1789, when Sen. William Maclay—who maintained an invaluable diary of proceedings in the Senate—was absent. The account was recorded by Benjamin Lincoln Lear, only son of GW's secretary Tobias Lear, in a letter to publishers Gales and Seaton, dated March 12, 1818, two years after the suicide of his father. Stephen Decatur, Jr., quotes the letter at length in his *Private Affairs of George Washington, From the Records and Accounts of Tobias Lear, Esquire, his Secretary* (Boston, 1933), 58-59; GW to the U.S. Senate, August 6, 1789, *PGW*, PS 3: 391-93.
18. GW to Moustier, May 25, 1789, *PGW*, PS 2: 389-91. For an insightful treatment of James Madison's role in shaping the administration during the early stages of GW's presidency, see Stuart Leibiger, *Founding Friendship: George Washington, James Madison, and the Creation of the American Republic* (Charlottesville, Va., 1999).
19. GW to James Anderson, December 21, 1797, GW to James McHenry, July 13, 1796, John C. Fitzpatrick, ed., *The Writings of George Washington, from the Original Manuscript Sources, 1745-1799*, 39 vols. (Washington, D.C., 1931-44), [cited herafter as Fitzpatrick, ed., *Writings of Washington*] 36: 110-14, 35: 136-38.

20. For Jefferson's Cabinet Circular, November 6, 1801, see Thomas Jefferson to GW, April 1, 1790, *PGW*, PS 5: 302-3, note 1. The word "gestion," used by Jefferson in this passage, means "management" or "conduct".

21. GW to Edmund Randolph, February 11, 1790, *PGW*, PS 5: 131-32.

22. GW to John Adams, May 10, 1789, *PGW*, PS 2: 245-50.

23. GW to David Stuart, July 26, 1789, *PGW*, PS 3: 321-27; GW to Alexander Hamilton, July 2, 1794, Fitzpatrick, ed., *Writings of Washington*, 33: 420-22.

CHAPTER TWO

24. GW to David Stuart, March 28, 1790, *PGW*, PS 5: 286-88.

25. Alexander Hamilton, Report on Manufactures, Harold C. Syrett, ed., *The Papers of Alexander Hamilton,* 27 vols. (New York, 1967-87), 10: 266-67; see also Forrest McDonald, *Alexander Hamilton: A Biography* (New York, 1979), 234.

26. See, e.g., GW's comments on the assumption of state debts in his letter to David Stuart of June 15, 1790, *PGW*, PS 5: 523-28.

27. GW to the chevalier de Chastellux, October 15, 1783, Fitzpatrick, ed., *Writings of Washington*, 27: 188-90.

28. Gordon S. Wood, *The Radicalism of the American Revolution* (New York, 1993), 34-36.

29. GW to Thomas Jefferson, March 29, 1784, GW to Benjamin Harrison, October 10, 1784, *PGW*, CS 1: 237-41, CS 2: 86-98.

30. GW to Lafayette, August 15, 1786, *PGW*, CS 4: 214-16.

31. The case for GW as a devotee of urban commercial society is ably made in John Ferling, *The First of Men: A Life of George Washington* (Knoxville, Tenn., 1988), 416-20; for GW's comments on the "vast progress" being made in the New England and the Middle States, see GW to La Luzerne, September 10, 1791, *PGW*, PS 8: 517-18; for GW's preference for northern schools, see, e.g., GW to William A. Washington, February 18, 1795, Fitzpatrick, ed., *Writings of Washington*, 34: 119-20.

32. GW to Lafayette, January 29, 1789, *PGW*, PS 1: 262-63; John R. Nelson, Alexander Hamilton and American Manufacturing: A Reexamination," *Journal of American History*, 65 (1979), 971-95.

33. GW to Gouverneur Morris, July 28, 1791, GW to David Humphreys, July 20, 1791, *PGW*, PS 8: 381-84, 358-61.

34. Jefferson's "Anas," July 10, 1792, Paul L. Ford, ed., *The Writings of Thomas Jefferson,* 12 vols. (New York, 1904), 1: 227-31.

CHAPTER THREE

35. GW to Benjamin Harrison, October 10, 1784, *PGW*, CS 2: 86-98.

36. ibid.

37. GW to William Moultrie, February 10, 1793, Fitzpatrick, ed., *Writings of Washington* 32: 337-38.

38. GW to the United States Senate, Aug. 11, 1790, *PGW*, PS 6: 237-39.

39. William Henry Smith, ed., *The St. Clair Papers: The Life and Public Service of Arthur St. Clair,* 2 vols. (Cincinnati, 1882), 2: 260-61. For a detailed account of the campaign, see Wiley Sword, *President Washington's Indian War: The Struggle for the Old Northwest* (Norman, Oklahoma, 1985), 145-203.

40. For the congressional debates on this issue see Gales, *Debates and Proceeedings of the Second Congress*, 337-55

41. Benjamin Hawkins to GW, 10 February 1792, *PGW*, PS 9: 554-559. "Errors of Government Towards the Indians," [February, 1792], Fitzpatrick, ed., *Writings of Washington*, 31: 491-94.

42 James Madison to Henry Lee, April 15, 1792, Robert Rutland, ed., *The Papers of James Madison*, First Series, 17 vols. (Chicago and Charlottesville, 1962-1991), 14: 287-88.

43. GW to Henry Knox, August 19, 1792, Fitzpatrick, ed., *Writings of Washington*, 32: 117-24.

44. GW to Henry Knox, August 22, 1792, Fitzpatrick, ed., *Writings of Washington*, 32: 125-28.

45. On the population explosion and the westward shift in the American population, see Wood, *Radicalism of the American Revolution*, 308-10.

CHAPTER FOUR

46. Kenneth Bowling, *Creation of Washington, D.C—The Idea and Location of the American Capital* (Fairfax, Va., 1991) [cited hereafter as Bowling, *Creation of Washington, D.C.*] 195.

47. Commission, Jan. 22, 1791, *PGW*, PS 7: 258-60; for a detailed discussion of these appointments and later ones, see William C. di Giacomantonio, "All the Presidents Men: George Washington's Federal City Commissioners.," *Washington History*, 3 (Spring-Summer 1991) 52-75.

48. Bowling, *Creation of Washington, D.C.,* 237-38, 214. Variations of GW's name, including "Washingtonople" and "Washingtonopolis" had been suggested earlier, so the decision to name the city for GW was not unexpected. The commissioners named the District of Columbia at the same meeting.

49. Pierre L'Enfant to GW, August 19, 1791, *PGW,* PS 8: 439-448.

50. See GW to Thomas Jefferson, January 2, 1791, editorial note, *PGW,* PS 7: 161-68. This land development scheme was first suggested by George Walker, one of the proprietors.

51. See Pierre L'Enfant to GW, Febraury 28, 1791, *PGW,* PS 9: 604-6.

52. GW to the Commissioners of the District of Columbia, January 31, 1793, Fitzpatrick, ed., *Writings of Washington,* 32: 324-25.

53. GW to Tobias Lear, September 25, 1793, GW to Arthur Young, December 12, 1793, Fitzpatrick, ed., *Writings of Washington,* 33: 104-6, 174-83.

54. Richard Norton Smith, *Patriarch: George Washington and the New American Nation* (Boston, 1993), 267.

55. Rochefoucauld quoted in Elizabeth S. Kite, *L'Enfant and Washington, 1791-1792* (Baltimore, 1929), 28; Benjamin Henry Latrobe to Phillip Mazzei, May 29, 1806, John C. Van Horne and Lee W. Formwalt, eds., *The Papers of Benjamin Henry Latrobe: Correspondence and Miscellaneous Papers,* 3 vols. (New Haven, 1984-88), 2: 227-28.

56. GW to William Thornton, December 8, 1799, Fitzpatrick, ed., *Writings of Washington,* 37: 455-56.

57. John Randolph to Albert Gallatin, June 28, 1805, Hannah Gallatin to Albert Gallatin, June 5, 1804, Gallatin Papers, New York Historical Society.

58. Frances Trollope, quoted in James Sterling Young, *The Washington Community, 1800-1828* (New York, 1966), 24; Jean-Jacques Ampere, quoted in Kite, *L'Enfant and Washington,* 28.

59. GW to Sarah Cary Fairfax, May 16, 1798, W. W. Abbot, ed., *PGW,* Retirement Series, 4 vols. (Charlottesville, Va., 1998-99) 2: 272-75.

CHAPTER FIVE

60. Marshall Smelser, "The Federalist Period as an Age of Passion," *American Quarterly,* 10 (Winter, 1958), 239-58; John R. Howe, Jr., "Republican Thought and Political Violence of the 1790s," *American Quarterly,* 10 (Summer, 1967), 147-65.

61. This interpretation of Hamilton's purpose owes much to Forrest McDonald, *Alexander Hamilton: A Biography* (New York, 1979); for a contrasting interpretation of Hamilton as a defender of the traditional hierarchies whose goal was the creation of a powerful fiscal-military state, see Wood, *Radicalism of the American Revolution,* 262-65.

62. Jefferson to James Madison, June 20, 1787, Julian Boyd, *et al* eds., *The Papers of Thomas Jefferson,* 27 vols. to date (Princeton, 1950 -), 11: 482. *See also* Robert Wiebe, *The Opening of American Society* (New York, 1984), 52-54.

63. GW to Arthur Fenner, June 4, 1790, *PGW,* PS 5: 470.

64. First Inaugural Address, *PGW,* PS 2: 173-77; Ralph Ketcham, *Presidents Above Party: The First American Presidency, 1789-1829* (Chapel Hill, 1984), 55-68.

65. Memoranda of Conversations with the President, March 1, 1792, Charles Cullen, ed., *Papers of Thomas Jefferson,* 23: 184-88.

66. Alexander Hamilton to GW, July 30, 1792, PGW, PS 10 (forthcoming).

67. Thomas Jefferson to GW, May 23, 1792 (second letter), Charles Cullen, ed., *Papers of Thomas Jefferson,* 23: 535-41.

68. Jefferson's "Anas," July 10, 1792, Ford, ed., *Writings of Thomas Jefferson,* 1: 227-31.

69. GW to Alexander Hamilton, 29 July 1792, Fitzpatrick, ed., *Writings of Washington,* 32: 95-100; Forrest McDonald, *Alexander Hamilton: A Biography,* 252, argues that GW was seeking a point-by-point rebuttal of Jefferson's charges to use in the future.

70. GW to Thomas Jefferson, August 23, 1792, GW to Alexander Hamilton, August 26, 1792, and GW to Edmund Randolph, August 26, 1792, Fitzpatrick, ed., *Writings of Washington,* 32: 129-32, 132-34, 135-37.

71. Alexander Hamilton to GW, September 9, 1792, Harold Syrett, ed., *The Papers of Alexander Hamilton,* 26 vols. (New York, 1961-79), 12: 347-49.

72. Thomas Jefferson to GW, September 9, 1792, John Catanzariti, ed., *Papers of Thomas Jefferson,* 24: 351-59.

73. Edmund Randolph to GW, August 5, 1792, George Washington Papers, Library of Congress.

74. John Taylor, *An Argument Respecting the Constitutionality of the Carriage Tax* (Richmond, 1795), 78-79.

75. GW to Henry Lee, August 26, 1794, GW to John Jay, November 1, 1794, and GW to Edmund Randolph, October 16, 1794, Fitzpatrick, ed., *Writings of Washington,* 33: 474-79, 34: 15-19, 2-4.

76. Dumas Malone, *Jefferson and the Ordeal of Liberty* (Boston, 1962), 188-89; Thomas Jefferson to James Monroe, May 26, 1795, Ford, ed., *Writings of Thomas Jefferson*, 8: 176-82; William Findley, *History of the Insurrection in the Western Parts of Pennsylvania in the Year 1794* (Philadelphia, 1795), 187.

77. GW to Thomas Jefferson, July 6 1796, Fitzpatrick, ed., *Writings of Washington*, 35: 118-22.

CHAPTER SIX

78. GW to Michel St. Jean de Crévecoeur, April 10, 1789, *PGW*, PS 2: 43-44; An opponent of the French Revolution, the vicomte de Chateaubriand, saw the key in GW's presidential house in Philadelphia. He was skeptical of the authenticity of the relic and the significance of Lafayette's tribute. "The keys of the Bastille multiplied," he commented. "They were sent to all the important simpletons in the four quarters of the world." If GW had seen the mob that stormed the Bastille "disporting themselves in the gutters of Paris," Chateaubriand was certain that "he would have felt less respect for his relic" (Chateaubriand, *Memoirs,* 6 vols. [New York, 1906], 1: 158, 211).

79. GW to Gouverneur Morris, October 13, 1789, *PGW*, PS 4: 176-79.

80. Gouverneur Morris to GW, February 4, 1792, *PGW*, PS 9: 531-40.

81. Thomas Jefferson to James Madison, June 23, 1793, John Catanzariti, ed., *Papers of Thomas Jefferson*, 26: 346.

82. Thomas Jefferson to James Monroe, August 9, 1788, Julian Boyd, ed., *Papers of Thomas Jefferson*, 13: 489; Thomas Jefferson to James Madison, April 28, 1793, John Catanzariti, ed., *Papers of Thomas Jefferson*, 25: 619-20.

83. GW to Henry Laurens, November 14, 1778, Fitzpatrick, ed., *Writings of Washington*, 13: 254-57; the centrality of this idea in GW's thinking about international relations is most ably described in Edmund S. Morgan, *The Genius of George Washington* (Washington, D.C., 1980).

84. GW to Edward Newenham, August 29, 1788, *PGW*, CS 6: 486-89.

85. Notes of Cabinet Meeting on Edmond Charles Genet, August 2, 1793, John Catanzariti, ed., *Papers of Thomas Jefferson*, 26: 601-3.

86. Frederick Jackson Turner, ed., "Correspondence of the French Ministers to the United States, 1791-1797," *Annual Report of the American Historical Association for the Year 1902,* 2 vols. (Washington, D.C., 1904), 2: 201-11.

87. Jefferson and the American Debt to France, editorial note, Jefferson to Genet, June 11, 1793, and Genet to Jefferson, June 18, 1793, John Catanzariti, ed., *Papers of Thomas Jefferson*, 26: 174-84, 252, 308-12.

88. GW to the U.S. Senate and House of Representatives, December 5, 1793, Fitzpatrick, ed., *Writings of Washington*, 33: 170-73.

89. Memorandum on Meeting of March 12, 1794, Charles R. King, ed., *The Life and Correspondence of Rufus King*, 6 vols. (New York, 1894-1900), 1: 518.

90. GW to Alexander Hamilton, July 29, 1795, Fitzpatrick, ed., *Writings of Washington*, 34: 262-64.

91. Stanley Elkins and Eric McKitrick, *The Age of Federalism* (New York, 1993), 382, 411.

92. GW to Patrick Henry, October 9, 1795, Fitzpatrick, ed., *Writings of Washington*, 34: 334-35.

EPILOGUE

93. GW to Benjamin Lincoln, October 26, 1788, *PGW*, PS 1: 70-74.

94. The text of the Farewell Address is in Fitzpatrick, ed., *Writings of Washington*, 35: 214-38, and is conveniently reprinted as an appendix in Matthew Spalding and Patrick Garrity, *A Sacred Union of Citizens: George Washington's Farewell Address and the American Character* (Lanham, Md., 1994).

95. Spalding and Garrity, *A Sacred Union of Citizens*, 137.

96. Jacob C. Parsons, ed., *Extracts from the Diary of Jacob Hiltzheimer of Philadelphia* (Philadelphia, 1893), 234; Fisher Ames to Oliver Wolcott September 26, 1796, William B. Allen, ed., *Works of Fisher Ames*, 2: 1192.

97. James Madison to James Monroe, September 29, 1796, Robert Rutland, ed., *Papers of James Madison*, 16: 403.

98. GW to the Pennsylvania Legislature, September 12, 1789, *PGW*, PS 4: 23-25.

99. John Adams to Abigail Adams, March 5, 1797, Charles Francis Adams, ed., *Letters of John Adams, Addressed to His Wife* (Boston, 1841), 2: 244.

100. John Carroll and Mary Ashworth, *George Washington: First in Peace* (New York, 1957), 438.

101. GW to the Pennsylvania Legislature, September 12, 1789, *PGW*, PS 4: 23-25.

SUGGESTIONS FOR FURTHER READING

ALL SERIOUS STUDENTS OF THE WASHINGTON presidency should acquaint themselves with the vast array of primary sources on early national politics now being published in definitive scholarly editions. The most important on Washington's presidency is *The Papers of George Washington*, Presidential Series (Charlottesville, Va. 1987-), edited by Dorothy A. Twohig, Mark A. Mastromarino, and Jack D. Warren, Jr., and published by the University Press of Virginia. This edition, which is co-sponsored by the Mount Vernon Ladies' Association of the Union, is the first to include Washington's incoming as well as his outgoing correspondence. Nine of an anticipated twenty-four volumes of Washington's presidential papers have been published since 1987, documenting the period from October 1788 to February 1792. Most of Washington's outgoing correspondence for the years 1792-97 can be found in volumes 31-35 of John C. Fitzpatrick's edition of *The Writings of George Washington,* 39 vols. (Washington, D.C., 1931-44).

Of comparable importance are Harold Syrett, ed., *The Papers of Alexander Hamilton,* 26 vols. (New York, 1961-79) and Julian P. Boyd, Charles Cullen, and John Catanzariti, eds., *The Papers of Thomas Jefferson,* 27 vols. to date (Princeton, 1950-). Of particular importance for the first years of the Washington presidency is Charlene Bickford, Kenneth Bowling, Helen Veit, and William C. diGiacomantonio, eds., *The Documentary History of the First Federal Congress,* 14 vols. to date (Baltimore, 1972-).

There have been surprisingly few specialized studies of the Washington presidency. The most widely known, Forrest McDonald, *The Presidency of George Washington* (Lawrence, Kansas, 1974), underestimates Washington's importance as an executive leader in his own administration, and focuses largely on the conduct of Alexander Hamilton and to a lesser extent, Thomas Jefferson. Richard Norton Smith, *Patriarch: George Washington and the New American Nation* (Boston, 1993), offers an engaging narrative account of Washington's presidential years.

Most Washington biographers have devoted more attention to the Revolutionary War than to Washington's presidency. Douglas Southall Freeman, whose monumental seven-volume biography remains the finest life of Washington yet written, did not live to carry his narrative of the Washington presidency beyond the first term. The final volume, completed by John Carroll and Mary Ashworth, is thorough, but lacks the insights Freeman might have provided. The treatment in James T. Flexner's four-volume *George Washington* (Boston, 1965-72), is gracefully written and focuses more attention on Washington's personality and private life. Casual readers will enjoy Flexner's one-volume treatment, *Washington, The Indispensable Man* (New York, 1974). John Ferling, *The First of Men: A Life of George Washington* (Knoxville, Tenn., 1988), is the work of a perceptive critic whose interpretations of Washington's conduct are often insightful if not always flattering.

The best treatment of the first decade of national politics can be found in

Stanley Elkins and Eric McKitrick, *The Age of Federalism* (New York, 1993). John C. Miller, *The Federalist Era, 1789-1801* (New York, 1960), remains the best brief account of national politics in the 1790s. Gordon S. Wood, *The Radicalism of the American Revolution* (New York, 1992), offers a sweeping interpretation of the transforming consequences of the American Revolution that places the political events of the 1790s in the broader context of emerging democratic culture.

John Chester Miller, *Alexander Hamilton: Portrait in Paradox* (New York, 1959), is perhaps the most balanced biography of Washington's treasury secretary. The most insightful is Forrest McDonald, *Alexander Hamilton: A Biography* (New York, 1979). McDonald underestimates Washington's political skill, but he combines a nuanced portrait of Hamilton's intellectual development with a mastery of the financial issues that confronted him. Richard Brookhiser, *Alexander Hamilton: American* (New York, 1999), is a gracefully written character study. Noble Cunningham, *In Pursuit of Reason: The Life of Thomas Jefferson* (Baton Rouge, La., 1987), and Merrill Peterson, *Thomas Jefferson and the New Nation: A Biography* (New York, 1970), are thorough one-volume biographies of Washington's first secretary of state. Joseph Ellis, *American Sphinx: The Character of Thomas Jefferson* (New York, 1997), offers valuable insights into Jefferson's conduct in Washington's administration.

Among more specialized monographs, Leonard White, *The Federalists: A Study in Administrative History, 1789-1801* (New York, 1948), remains the most comprehensive study of the administrative practices adopted by Washington and his department heads. Dale Van Every, *Ark of Empire: The American Frontier, 1784-1804* (New York, 1963), offers an engaging account of Washington's patient prosecution of war and diplomacy in the West. The early history of the Federal City has only recently begun to attract the attention it deserves. Kenneth Bowling, *The Creation of Washington, D.C.— The Idea and Location of the American Capital* (Fairfax, Va., 1991), presents an insightful scholarly analysis of the movement that culminated in the placement of the city on the Potomac. Bob Arnebeck, *Through a Fiery Trial: Building Washington, 1790-1800* (Lanham, Md., 1991), offers an entertaining popular account of the development of the city during its first decade. The best brief analysis of the ideas that underlay Washington's foreign policy is in Edmund S. Morgan, *The Genius of George Washington* (New York, 1980). The relative roles of Washington and Hamilton in formulating the Farewell Address has been the subject of a great deal of discussion. Most recent scholars interpret the address as an expression of Washington's ideas, to which Hamilton made important contributions, while Washington acted as final editor of the whole. This view has been advanced most recently in Mathew Spalding and Patrick J. Garrity, *A Sacred Union of Citizens: George Washington's Farewell Address and the American Character* (Lanham, Md., 1996).

List of Illustrations

INDEX

Congress, U.S. (1789-present): and Indian war, 41, 42, 45; and GW's appointments, 13-16; and GW's inauguration, 5; and public debt, 22, 23, 24-28, 65, 66; and Neutrality Proclamation, 83, 85-86; and seat of government, 51-53, 54-55, 58; and Whiskey Rebellion, 72; convenes, 1; relations with GW, 13-19. *See also* Excise Act; House of Representatives, U.S.; Neutrality Act; Residence Act; Senate, U.S.

Constitution, 1, 2, 3, 9, 15, 17-18, 21, 61, 65, 72, 73, 81, 86, 87, 88, 91: *See also* Presidency.

Constitutional Convention (1787), 10, 21, 23

Continental Army, 2, 9, 13, 41

Conway, Richard, 2

Creek (Indians), 37, 38-40

Crevecœur, Michael St. Jean de, 76

Cumberland, Md., 59

Cumberland River, 44

Custis, John Parke, 53

Democratic Societies, 71, 72, 73

Detroit (British fort), 35

District of Columbia: commissioners for, 53, 54, 56, 58; location of, 52, 53; name of, 99; topography of, 53. *See also* Washington, D.C.

Dorchester, Lord: *See* Carleton, Guy, Lord Dorchester

East Florida, 36

Eastern Branch (of the Potomac River), 53, 54

Eel River, 40

Erie Canal, 58

Evans, Oliver, 30

Excise Act, 26, 70-72

Fairfax, Sarah (Sally), 59

Fallen Timbers, Battle of, 46, 47

Farewell Address (1796), 66, 91-94

Federal City: *See* Washington, D.C.

Federal Constitution: *See* Constitution

Federalist, The, 23

Fenno, John, 65

Findley, William, 72

Fishbourn, Benjamin, 15-16

Florida (East and West), 36, 82

Fort Washington (Ohio), 40, 41, 44

Fort Wayne, Ind., 40

France: administrative system of, 14; alliance with the U.S., 81; and GW's "Farewell Address," 94; and the Ohio Valley, 37; Constituent Assembly, 76; Declaration of the Rights of Man and the Citizen, 76; National Assembly, 76, 77; Treaty of Amity and Commerce with, 81; U.S. debt to, 21, 82; U.S. minister to, 15, 16, 19; U.S. trade with, 87; war with Britain (1793), 44, 69. *See also* French and Indian War; French Revolution

French and Indian War, 37, 42-43, 50

French Revolution, 75-85

Freneau, Philip, 65, 81

Gallatin, Albert, 58

Gallatin, Hannah, 58

Genet, Edmond, 81-83, 85

Genet, Cornelia Clinton, 83

ABOUT THE AUTHOR

Jack D. Warren, Jr., is an historian and writer whose work on George Washington has appeared in numerous popular publications, including *The Washington Post*. He served as an Assistant Editor of *The Papers of George Washington* at the University of Virginia from 1993 to 1998 and is the author of several scholarly monographs on Washington. He is currently the historical advisor to George Washington Birthplace National Monument and the George Washington House Project of the Barbados National Trust. He lives in La Plata, Maryland, with his wife, Janet, and their children Emily, Audrey, and Jack D. Warren, III.